SECOND FORM LATIN

CHERYL LOWE

W9-BRP-770

SECOND FORM LATIN
STUDENT TEXT
by Cheryl Lowe

Published by:
Memoria Press
www.MemoriaPress.com

First Edition © 2010 by Memoria Press Copyright
All rights reserved
ISBN #978-1-61538-023-7

Cover image: Caesar Crossing the Rubicon

No part of this book may be reproduced in any form by any means
without written permission from the publisher.

Magistris et Discipulis

(To Teachers and Students)

Second Form Latin continues the study of the Latin grammar in much the same format as *First Form Latin*. The Units are organized in a logical, systematic order that maximizes understanding and retention. Every lesson contains a digestible bit of material that can be understood and mastered in one week. Every effort has been made to enable the student to continue his march through the Latin grammar without being overwhelmed and frustrated.

All material in *First Form Latin* is reviewed in this text in the following four lessons:

Lesson 1	1st/2nd declension nouns and adjectives
Lesson 4	Declensions 3-5
Lesson 12	1st/2nd conjugations and **sum**, present system
Lesson 17	1st/2nd conjugations and **sum**, perfect system

The dative and genitive cases are introduced in the first unit, and prepositions in the second unit, all of which allow for greater variety in sentence structure. Sentences are designed for skills practice rather than for the development of connected text. Likewise, vocabulary is chosen and arranged to maximize retention, rather than for the purpose of developing a story line. Sentences that students can translate without frustration build confidence and pleasure in Latin reading.

Because students have learned the basics of Latin and how it works, *Second Form Latin* in many ways is easier to teach and learn than *First Form*. The only *caveat* is the problem of retaining previously learned material while continually adding new. Languages, whether mathematical or verbal, are cumulative and that is what makes them difficult. Everything must be remembered and nothing can be forgotten. There *is* a solution to this problem: consistent daily review consisting of both oral recitation and written exercises. Continual review is the key to success in Latin. The importance of mastery learning cannot be overemphasized.

There are some major milestones in your Latin journey this year. I hope you are excited about continuing your climb up the mountain of Latin grammar. At the end of this book you will be halfway there!

Dominus vobiscum,
Cheryl Lowe

Contents

Roman Couple

These two well-to-do young Romans—possibly a couple or, more likely, brother and sister—were painted in fresco on the wall of a house in Pompeii. She holds a writing tablet and stylus, and he holds a scroll. These implements, the attire, and the expressions of the pair all show the sophistication of Roman culture of the time.

Pronunciation

In *First Form Latin* students learned the basics of Latin pronunciation. In this second year, students should be required to observe the accent marks when reading Latin silently or aloud. The accent marks are there to help the student know which syllable to accent. They do not need to be reproduced in written work. The rule for pronunciation is extremely simple. Accent the next last syllable (penult) unless you see an accent mark on the second last syllable (antepenult). Review Accents on the next page with students.

For oral recitation time, however, you may want to continue accenting the inflected ending rather than the accented syllable. Students need reinforcement in learning grammar endings, which is the purpose of the oral recitation.

Alphabet

The Latin alphabet has the same letters as English except that it has no **w**. The letters **y, z,** and **k** are infrequent and usually found in words of Greek origin. The Roman letter **i** was both a vowel and a consonant (similar to the English **y**). The letter **j** was added during the Middle Ages for consonantal **i.** Thus **Iulius** and **Iesus** came to be written **Julius** and **Jesus.**

Vowels

Latin has long and short vowels, but the distinction between them is not always observed by English speakers. In this text, we will focus on learning the long vowels and the consonants only. You will notice on the audio some vowels that tend toward the short sounds, so the short vowel sounds are given below. In this text, long vowels will not be marked with a macron except for a few inflected endings.

long	as in	sound	example	short	as in	sound	example
ā	f*a*ther	/ah/	**frāter**	a	*a*gain	/uh/	**mensa**
ē	l*a*te	/ā/ or /ay/	**sēdēs**	e	*E*d	/ĕ/	**et**
ī	s*ee*n	/ē/ or /ee/	**amīcus**	i	*i*t	/ĭ/	**cibus**
ō	*o*pen	/ō/ or /oh/	**nōmen**	o	*o*n	/ŏ/	**novem**
ū	f*oo*d	/o͞o/	**lūna**	u	f*oo*t	/o͝o/	**sum**

A helpful tip to remember the five long vowels is to learn the two words, **gloria** and **Jesu.**

The general rule for consecutive and double vowels is to give each vowel its proper sound with the following exceptions:

Digraphs		as in	sound	example
	ae and **oe**	l*a*te	/ā/	**caelum, proelium**
Diphthong				
	au	*ou*t	/ou/	**laudo**

Consonants

The Latin consonants have the same sounds as in English except as noted below. The rules for hard and soft **c** and **g** are usually true in English and always true in Latin. Note that soft **c** and **sc** have different sounds in English and Latin.

c, g, and **sc** are hard before **a, o, u,** and **consonants**

hard **c** as in **c**at	/k/	**culpa, clamo**
hard **g** as in **g**o	/g/	**fuga, gloria**
hard **sc** as in **sc**out	/sk/	**scutum**

c, g, and **sc** are soft before **e, i, ae, oe**

soft **c** as in **ch**arity	/ch/	**caelum**
soft **g** as in **g**em	/j/	**regina**
soft **sc** as in **sh**out	/sh/	**scio**

gn as in canyon	/ny/	**pugno**
ch is hard as in chemistry	/k/	**choro**
j as in yes	/y/	**juvo**

s as in **s**ing, never as in nose /z/	/s/	**mensa**

t when followed by **i** and another vowel	/tsee/	**gratia**

Accents

For the beginning Latin student, the most helpful information is not long and short vowels, but rather knowing what syllable to accent. In this text, you will always know the accented syllable by following these easy rules. The last three syllables in a Latin word have names.

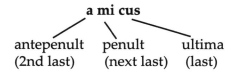

a mi cus

antepenult   penult   ultima
(2nd last)   (next last)   (last)

Latin words are always accented on either the penult or the antepenult, never on the last syllable. In this text, if the accent is on the penult, it will not have an accent mark, but if the accent is on the antepenult, it will have an accent mark.

a*mi*cus   but   á*m*bulo

accent on the penult - no mark   *accent on the antepenult - accent mark*

♦ In *First Form* you learned all five declensions and 1st/2nd declension adjectives. Now you are ready to learn some variations that occur in these declensions. Learning a few exceptions is easy after you have learned the basic rules.

♦ In this Unit you will first review 1st and 2nd declension nouns and adjectives and then learn about **er-ir** nouns and adjectives of the 2nd declension masculine.

♦ Most 2nd declension masculine nouns end in **us** in the nominative singular, but there are a few that end in **er** and one that ends in **ir**. These masculine nouns are declined with the same case endings you have already learned.

♦ You will also review declensions 3-5 and learn about 3rd declension i-stem nouns and 3rd declension adjectives.

♦ 3rd declension **i-stem** nouns are a large group that deviate slightly from the regular 3rd declension nouns.

♦ There are only two types of adjectives in Latin:
     1st/2nd declension adjectives
     3rd declension adjectives

♦ You learned 1st/2nd declension adjectives in *First Form*, and you will learn 3rd declension adjectives in this unit.

♦ In *First Form* you learned to use the nominative and accusative cases. In this unit you will be introduced to the genitive and dative cases.

UNIT I

Nouns - Adjectives

The Appian Way

All roads lead to Rome. The Appian Way, initiated by Appius Claudius, was the great road between Rome and the port of Brindisi, the gateway to Greece and the East. Rome's magnificent system of roads made communication, commerce, and rapid movement of troops possible, and by them Rome maintained control over her far-flung empire. Built by the legions with superb engineering, they were resistant to freezing and flooding and required little maintenance. Like *Roma Eterna*, they were built to last for the ages.

First Form Review

First and Second Declension Nouns

Case	1st Declension S.	1st Declension Pl.	2nd Declension Masculine S.	2nd Declension Masculine Pl.	2nd Declension Neuter S.	2nd Declension Neuter Pl.
nom.	mensa	mensae	servus	servi	bellum	bella
gen.	mensae	mensarum	servi	servorum	belli	bellorum
dat.	mensae	mensis	servo	servis	bello	bellis
acc.	mensam	mensas	servum	servos	bellum	bella
abl.	mensā	mensis	servo	servis	bello	bellis

First and Second Declension Adjectives

Case	Singular M.	Singular F.	Singular N.	Plural M.	Plural F.	Plural N.
nom.	bonus	bona	bonum	boni	bonae	bona
gen.	boni	bonae	boni	bonorum	bonarum	bonorum
dat.	bono	bonae	bono	bonis	bonis	bonis
acc.	bonum	bonam	bonum	bonos	bonas	bona
abl.	bono	bonā	bono	bonis	bonis	bonis

Numbers

Roman Numerals	Cardinal		Ordinal	
I	unus -a -um	one	primus -a -um	first
II	duo	two	secundus -a -um	second
III	tres	three	tértius -a -um	third
IV	quattuor	four	quartus -a -um	fourth
V	quinque	five	quintus -a -um	fifth
VI	sex	six	sextus -a -um	sixth
VII	septem	seven	séptimus -a -um	seventh
VIII	octo	eight	octavus -a -um	eighth
IX	novem	nine	nonus -a -um	ninth
X	decem	ten	décimus -a -um	tenth

Vocabulary Review

aeternus -a -um	eternal everlasting	**equus -i** *m.*	horse	**parvus -a -um**	small
agnus -i *m.*	lamb	**fílius -i** *m.*	son	**poeta -ae** *m.*	poet
agrícola -ae *m.*	farmer	**forum -i** *n.*	forum, marketplace	**puella -ae** *f.*	girl
altus -a -um	high, deep	**Itália -ae** *f.*	Italy	**regina -ae** *f.*	queen
amicus -i *m.*	friend	**latus -a -um**	wide, broad	**regnum -i** *n.*	kingdom
annus -i *m.*	year	**magnus -a -um**	great, large	**Roma -ae** *f.*	Rome
bellum -i *n.*	war	**malus -a -um**	bad	**sanctus -a -um**	sacred, holy
bonus -a -um	good	**Maria -ae** *f.*	Mary	**saxum -i** *n.*	rock
caelum -i *n.*	sky, heaven	**mensa -ae** *f.*	table	**servus -i** *m.*	slave, servant
Christus -i *m.*	Christ	**multus -a -um**	much, many	**templum -i** *n.*	temple
débitum -i *n.*	debt, sin	**mundus -i** *m.*	world, mankind	**terra -ae** *f.*	earth, land
deus -i *m.*	god	**nauta -ae** *m.*	sailor	**verbum -i** *n.*	word
dóminus -i *m.*	lord, master	**novus -a -um**	new		
donum -i *n.*	gift	**óppidum -i** *n.*	town		

Grammar Review

◆ Four gender rules: (1) **NG** (2) **1D F** (3) **2D us M** (4) **2D um N**

◆ The neuter rule: The nominative and accusative cases are the same and end in **a** in the plural.

◆ A verb agrees with its subject in person and number.

◆ An adjective agrees with its noun in gender, number, and case, and may precede or follow its noun.

◆ A predicate nominative follows a linking verb, renames the subject, and is in the nominative case. A predicate adjective follows a linking verb, describes the subject, and is in the nominative case.

◆ The genitive singular of a 1st declension noun is **-ae**, and of a 2nd declension noun is **-i**.

Latin Sayings

Roma Aeterna   **Anno Dómini (A.D.)**   **ante bellum**

Quattuor anni témpora   **Mater Italiae Roma**

Ager Vaticanus   *The Vatican Field*

Second Declension **er, ir** Nouns

vir viri *m.*   man

Case	S.	Pl.
nom.	*vir*	*vir***i**
gen.	*vir***i**	*vir***orum**
dat.	*vir***o**	*vir***is**
acc.	*vir***um**	*vir***os**
abl.	*vir***o**	*vir***is**

puer pueri *m.*   boy, child

Case	S.	Pl.
nom.	*puer*	*púer***i**
gen.	*púer***i**	*puer***orum**
dat.	*púer***o**	*púer***is**
acc.	*púer***um**	*púer***os**
abl.	*púer***o**	*púer***is**

ager agri *m.*   field, ground

Case	S.	Pl.
nom.	*ager*	*agr***i**
gen.	*agr***i**	*agr***orum**
dat.	*agr***o**	*agr***is**
acc.	*agr***um**	*agr***os**
abl.	*agr***o**	*agr***is**

Vocabulary

Latin	Gender	English	Derivative(s)
vir viri	*m.*	man	*virile*
puer púeri	*m.*	boy, child	*puerile*
vesper vésperi	*m.*	evening	*vespers*
ager agri	*m.*	field, ground	*agriculture*
culter cultri	*m.*	knife	*cutlery*
liber libri	*m.*	book	*library*
magister magistri	*m.*	teacher (male)	*magistrate, master*
magistra -ae	*f.*	teacher (female)	
líberi liberorum	*m.*	children	

♦ Most 2nd declension masculine nouns end in **us** in the nominative singular, but there are some that end in **er** and one that ends in **ir**. Except for the nominative singular, these nouns have the same case endings as all 2nd declension masculine nouns. The **er** nouns are all masculine.

♦ These nouns show why it is important to always learn the genitive singular. The nominative singular of most declensions can vary, but the genitive singular never varies. The genitive singular 1) identifies the declension the noun belongs to and 2) provides the stem.

♦ Looking at the genitive singular of **puer, vir,** and **vesper,** you see that the stem is the same as the nominative singular form.

♦ Looking at the genitive singular of **ager, culter, magister,** and **liber,** you see that the genitive singular form drops the letter **e**.

♦ **Liberi liberorum,** *children,* is a noun that is declined in the plural only. Do not confuse:

liber	**libri**	book
líberi	**liberorum**	children
líbero	**liberare**	to set free

The **Ager Vaticanus** on the west bank of the Tiber River was the 14th district of the ancient city of Rome. Low-lying and damp, it was considered unhealthy and was used as a cemetery until the emperor Caligula built a racetrack, later enlarged by Nero, in the **ager**. It was the site of the martyrdom of St. Peter and thus became the location of Vatican City and St. Peter's Basilica. The original church, built by Constantine in the 4th century over St. Peter's tomb, was torn down and replaced by the current St. Peter's, built in the 15th century and designed by Michelangelo. The colonnade and square were added by Bernini in the 16th century.

St. Peter's Basilica
Rome, Italy

Ad astra per áspera. *To the stars through difficulties.*

Second Declension **er** Adjectives

First and Second Declension Adjectives

Case	Singular			Plural		
	M.	**F.**	**N.**	**M.**	**F.**	**N.**
nom.	ínteger	íntegra	íntegrum	íntegri	íntegrae	íntegra
gen.	íntegri	íntegrae	íntegri	integrorum	integrarum	integrorum
dat.	íntegro	íntegrae	íntegro	íntegris	íntegris	íntegris
acc.	íntegrum	íntegram	íntegrum	íntegros	íntegras	íntegra
abl.	íntegro	íntegrā	íntegro	íntegris	íntegris	íntegris

◆ Most 1st/2nd declension adjectives are of the type **bonus -a -um**. There are some, however, that have the **er** masculine ending instead of **us**. Since nouns and adjectives with the **er** ending either drop or retain the final **e**, the dictionary form must be written out in full. The case endings for these adjectives are the same as those for all 1st/2nd declension adjectives.

◆ Study the vocabulary list carefully. Which adjectives retain the final **e** in the stem and which adjectives drop the final **e** in the stem?

Vocabulary

Latin	English	Derivative(s)
dexter dextra dextrum	right, right-hand	*dexterity, dextrous*
sinister sinistra sinistrum	left, left-hand	*sinister*
ínteger íntegra íntegrum	whole, uninjured	*integral, integer*
pulcher pulchra pulchrum	beautiful	*pulchritude*
sacer sacra sacrum	sacred	*sacred, sacrifice*
aeger aegra aegrum	sick, ill	
piger pigra pigrum	lazy	
asper áspera ásperum	sharp, harsh	*asperity*
miser mísera míserum	wretched	*miserable*
liber líbera líberum	free	*liberty*

◆ **Liber, libera, liberum** is an adjective. Do not confuse four similar words:

líbero, liberare, liberavi, liberatus	*verb*	to set free
liber, líbera, líberum	*adjective*	free
liber libri	*noun*	book
líberi liberorum	pl. *noun*	children

Dative of Indirect Object

◆ An indirect object is commonly found with verbs of **giving** or **telling**. Examples of giving and telling verbs are: **do, narro, nuntio, demonstro.**

◆ In English, the indirect object can be expressed two ways.
1) word order - the indirect object precedes the direct object

    SN   V-t   IO   A   DO
Mary gave Mark a rose.

2) a prepositional phrase beginning with **to** or **for**

    SN   V-t   A   DO   P   OP
Mary gave a rose to Mark.

This is Sentence Pattern #5. See p. 88 for labeling abbreviations and p. 94 for how to diagram an indirect object.

◆ In Latin the indirect object is expressed by the dative case. The word *dative* comes from the Latin word **do, dare, dedi, datus**, *to give*. Both sentences above are translated only one way in Latin— by the dative case. (**Marcus -i** Mark, **Marco** is the dative sing.)

      SN   IO   DO   V-t
Maria Marco rosam dedit.

◆ In Latin the location of the indirect object is not fixed, but as in English, it usually precedes the direct object.

> The phrase **ad astra per áspera** is one of many medieval and modern Latin slogans that use the phrase **ad astra** (*to the stars, to the heights of glory,* etc.). Great feats of accomplishment can only be attained through the difficulties of hard work and the struggles of life. **Ad astra per aspera** is the motto of the state of Kansas.

"Per ardua ad astra" - British Royal Air Force motto- (Poppa)

[1]**Doceo** takes two accusatives rather than a direct and indirect object.

means " Through hard work to the stars"

First Form Review

Third, Fourth and Fifth Declension Nouns

Case	3rd Declension M/F		3rd Declension Neuter	
	S.	Pl.	S.	Pl.
nom.	pater	patres	nomen	nómina
gen.	patris	patrum	nóminis	nóminum
dat.	patri	pátribus	nómini	nomínibus
acc.	patrem	patres	nomen	nómina
abl.	patre	pátribus	nómine	nomínibus

Case	4th Declension		5th Declension	
	S.	Pl.	S.	Pl.
nom.	portus	portūs	res	res
gen.	portūs	pórtuum	rei	rerum
dat.	pórtui	pórtibus	rei	rebus
acc.	portum	portūs	rem	res
abl.	portu	pórtibus	re	rebus

◆ Memorize the genitive singular of every Latin noun carefully. The genitive singular (1) identifies the declension of the noun and 2) provides the stem.

◆ All nouns whose genitive singular ends in **is** are 3rd declension nouns.

◆ All nouns whose genitive singular ends in **ūs** are 4th declension nouns.

◆ All nouns whose genitive singular ends in **ei** are 5th declension nouns.

◆ All neuter nouns obey the neuter rule: the nominative and accusative case forms are identical and end in **a** in the plural.

◆ Natural gender trumps all other gender rules.

◆ Gender rules: **4D M**   Most 4th declension nouns are masculine.
  5D F   Most 5th declension nouns are feminine.

◆ The direct object of a verb is in the accusative case.

◆ 1st/2nd declension adjectives can modify nouns in declensions 3-5. An adjective agrees with its noun in gender, number, and case, but not declension.

16

Vocabulary Review

adventus -ūs *m.*	arrival	**mater matris** *f.*	mother
canis canis *m., f.*	dog	**metus -ūs** *m.*	fear
caput cápitis *n.*	head	**miles mílitis** *m.*	soldier
cor cordis *n.*	heart	**mos moris** *m.*	custom
crux crucis *f.*	cross	**nomen nóminis** *n.*	name
dies -ei *m.*	day	**panis panis** *m.*	bread
domus -ūs *f.*	house, home	**pater patris** *m.*	father
dux ducis *m.*	leader	**pax pacis** *f.*	peace
exércitus -ūs *m.*	army	**pes pedis** *m.*	foot
fácies -ei *f.*	face	**portus -ūs** *m.*	harbor
fides -ei *f.*	faith, trust	**res -ei** *f.*	thing, matter, affair, business
flumen flúminis *n.*	river	**rex regis** *m.*	king
frater fratris *m.*	brother	**senatus -ūs** *m.*	senate
fructus -ūs *m.*	fruit	**sol solis** *m.*	sun
lacus -ūs *m.*	lake	**soror sororis** *f.*	sister
lex legis *f.*	law	**spes -ei** *f.*	hope
lumen lúminis *n.*	lamp	**spíritus -ūs** *m.*	spirit
lux lucis *f.*	light	**vox vocis** *f.*	voice
manus -ūs *f.*	hand		

Latin Sayings

alma mater
Pax Romana
Rex Regum

Caput Mundi
Senatus Populusque Romanus (S.P.Q.R.)
Carpe diem.

Mare Nostrum   *Our Sea*

Third Declension **i-stem** Nouns

pars partis *f.*   part, region

Case	S.	Pl.
nom.	*pars*	*part*es
gen.	*part*is	*párt*ium
dat.	*part*i	*párt*ibus
acc.	*part*em	*part*es
abl.	*part*e	*párt*ibus

mare maris *n.*   sea

Case	S.	Pl.
nom.	*mare*	*már*ia
gen.	*mar*is	*már*ium
dat.	*mar*i	*már*ibus
acc.	*mare*	*már*ia
abl.	*mar*i	*már*ibus

♦ There are a large number of M/F 3rd declension nouns called **i-stem** nouns. Look at the declensions of **pars, partis**. How does it differ from the model declensions of **lex** or **pater**?

♦ In M/F **i-stem** nouns the letter **i** appears in the genitive plural, otherwise the case endings are the same as those you have already learned.

♦ **Mare** is a 3rd declension **i-stem** neuter noun that follows the neuter rule. In addition to the genitive plural, the letter **i** appears in the ablative singular and nominative and accusative plural.

Vocabulary

Latin	Gender	English	Derivative(s)
civis civis	*m. or f.*	citizen	*civil, civilian, civic*
hostis hostis	*m. or f.*	enemy	*hostile, hostility*
navis navis	*f.*	ship	*naval, navy*
collis collis	*m.*	hill	
pons pontis	*m.*	bridge	*pontoon*
mons montis	*m.*	mountain	*Montana*
pars partis	*f.*	part, region	*partition*
urbs urbis	*f.*	city	*urban, suburbs*
gens gentis	*f.*	tribe	*Gentile*
mare maris	*n.*	sea	*marine*

◆ How do you know if a noun is an **i-stem**? Most **i-stem** nouns are one or two syllable words and 1) they have the same number of syllables in the nominative and genitive singular (**civis, civis**) *or* 2) the genitive singular stem ends in two consonants (gens, ge**nt** is).

Genitive of Possession

◆ In English, possession is expressed by the preposition **of** or **'s**.

The mother of Italy   and   Italy's mother

◆ In Latin, the genitive case is used to express *possession*, or more generally *belonging to*. The possessive noun usually precedes its noun but it may also follow it. The meaning is the same and may be translated with **'s** or **of** in English—whichever sounds best.

Mater Itáliae   or   **Italiae Mater**

◆ Many *of* expressions in English are translated by the genitive. These expressions may denote relationships other than possession, such as *part* or *description*.

part of the field	**pars agri**
fear of God	**metus Dei**
King of Kings	**Rex Regum**
Head of the World	**Caput Mundi**

> **Mare Nostrum.** This extraordinary statement of power and self-confidence is the name used by the Romans for the Mediterranean Sea during the late republican and empire eras. It reflects the fact that Rome controlled all the lands surrounding the Mediterranean, making it a virtual Roman lake.

Ars longa vita brevis.   *Art is long and life is short.*

3rd Declension Adjectives, Two Terminations

brevis -e   short, brief

Case	M/F		N	
	S.	Pl.	S.	Pl.
nom.	*brev***is**	*brev***es**	*brev***e**	*brév***ia**
gen.	*brev***is**	*brév***ium**	*brev***is**	*brév***ium**
dat.	*brev***i**	*brév***ibus**	*brev***i**	*brév***ibus**
acc.	*brev***em**	*brev***es**	*brev***e**	*brév***ia**
abl.	*brev***i**	*brév***ibus**	*brev***i**	*brév***ibus**

♦ This is the second adjective type in Latin. There are no 4th and 5th declension adjectives.

Vocabulary

Latin	English	Derivative(s)
brevis -e	short, brief	*brief, brevity*
fácilis -e	easy	*facility*
difficilis -e	difficult	*difficulty*
fortis -e	strong, brave	*fortitude, fort*
gravis -e	heavy, serious, severe	*gravity*
omnis -e	each, every (s.), all (pl.)	*omni-*
turpis -e	shameful, disgraceful	*turpitude*
dulcis -e	sweet, pleasant	*dulcimer*
fidelis -e	faithful	*fidelity*
nóbilis -e	noble	*nobility*

◆ Look at the dictionary form for these adjectives. If we wrote them in the same dictionary form as the 1st/2nd declension adjectives (**bonus -a -um**), we would write all three genders like this:

brevis (M)   brevis (F)   breve (N)

But since we know that the masculine and feminine forms are the same in the 3rd declension, the dictionary form is simplified to

brevis (M/F)   breve (N)   or   **brevis -e**

◆ Look at the declension of **brevis** in the masculine/feminine. What do you notice? The 3rd declension adjectives are obviously related to the **i-stem** nouns. The letter **i** appears in the genitive plural <u>and</u> the ablative singular.

◆ Look at the declension of **brevis** in the neuter. It is identical to the declension of the neuter noun **mare** in the previous lesson.

> **Ars longa vita brevis** is the first part of the Latin rendition of a Greek aphorism attributed to the physician Hippocrates. In the Greek original, the parts are reversed. The full aphorism is "Life is short, art (the task) is long, the critical moment is fleeting, taking action is risky, deciding is painful."

Oral Drill

1. **pax brevis**	1. all seas	
2. **reges fortes**	2. to/for brave men	
3. **fructus dulcis**	3. of the noble tribes	
4. **virum fortem**	4. faithful children	
5. **mons difficilis**	5. easy book (d.o.)	
6. **cives nóbiles**	6. in each bridge	
7. **agrorum dúlcium**	7. short evening	
8. **hosti turpi**	8. pleasant hills	
9. **oppida omnia**	9. of the shameful war	
10. **facies gravis**	10. strong cities	

Second Declension **er, ir** Nouns

Case	S.	Pl.	S.	Pl.	S.	Pl.
nom.	*puer*	*púer*i	*vir*	*vir*i	*ager*	*agr*i
gen.	*púer*i	*puer*orum	*vir*i	*vir*orum	*agr*i	*agr*orum
dat.	*púer*o	*púer*is	*vir*o	*vir*is	*agr*o	*agr*is
acc.	*púer*um	*púer*os	*vir*um	*vir*os	*agr*um	*agr*os
abl.	*púer*o	*púer*is	*vir*o	*vir*is	*agr*o	*agr*is

First and Second Declension **er** Adjectives

Case	Singular			Plural		
	M.	F.	N.	M.	F.	N.
nom.	*liber*	*líber*a	*líber*um	*líber*i	*líber*ae	*líber*a
gen.	*líber*i	*líber*ae	*líber*i	*liber*orum	*liber*arum	*liber*orum
dat.	*líber*o	*líber*ae	*líber*o	*liber*is	*líber*is	*líber*is
acc.	*líber*um	*líber*am	*líber*um	*líber*os	*líber*as	*líber*a
abl.	*líber*o	*liber*ā	*líber*o	*líber*is	*líber*is	*líber*is

Third Declension **i-stem** Nouns

Case	S.	Pl.	S.	Pl.
nom.	*pars*	*part*es	*mare*	*már*ia
gen.	*part*is	*párt*ium	*mar*is	*már*ium
dat.	*part*i	*párt*ibus	*mar*i	*már*ibus
acc.	*part*em	*part*es	*mare*	*már*ia
abl.	*part*e	*párt*ibus	*mar*i	*már*ibus

Third Declension Adjectives

Case	Singular		Plural	
	M./F.	N.	M./F.	N.
nom.	*brev*is	*brev*e	*brev*es	*brév*ia
gen.	*brev*is	*brev*is	*brév*ium	*brév*ium
dat.	*brev*i	*brev*i	*brév*ibus	*brév*ibus
acc.	*brev*em	*brev*e	*brev*es	*brév*ia
abl.	*brev*i	*brev*i	*brév*ibus	*brev*ibus

Vocabulary Review

aeger –gra –grum	sick, ill	**magister –tri** *m.*	teacher (*m.*)
ager –agri *m.*	field, ground	**magistra –ae** *f.*	teacher (*f.*)
asper –a –um	sharp, harsh	**mare maris** *n.*	sea
brevis –e	short, brief	**miser –a –um**	wretched
civis -is *m. or f.*	citizen	**mons montis** *m.*	mountain
collis –is *m.*	hill	**navis –is** *f.*	ship
culter –tri *m.*	knife	**nóbilis –e**	noble
dexter –tra –trum	right, right-hand	**omnis –e**	each, every, all
difficilis –e	difficult	**pars partis** *f.*	part, region
dulcis –e	sweet, pleasant	**piger –gra –grum**	lazy
fácilis –e	easy	**pons pontis** *m.*	bridge
fidelis –e	faithful	**puer –i** *m.*	boy, child
fortis –e	strong, brave	**pulcher –chra –chrum**	beautiful
gens gentis *f.*	tribe	**sacer –cra –crum**	sacred
gravis –e	heavy, serious, severe	**sinister –tra –trum**	left, left-hand
hostis –is *m. or f.*	enemy	**turpis –e**	shameful, disgraceful
ínteger –gra –grum	whole, uninjured	**urbs urbis** *f.*	city
liber –a –um	free	**vesper vésperi** *m.*	evening
liber –bri *m.*	book	**vir viri** *m.*	man
líberi –orum *m.*	children		

Latin Sayings

Ager Vaticanus
Mare Nostrum

Ad astra per áspera.
Ars longa vita brevis.

Introduction to Unit Two
Personal Pronouns, Prepositions

◆ A pronoun takes the place of a noun. The word the pronoun refers to or takes the place of is called the **antecedent**.

◆ There are eight kinds of pronouns. Learn these pronouns in pairs. See appendix for examples.
personal and **possessive**
reflexive and **intensive**
relative and **interrogative**
demonstrative and **indefinite**

◆ The pronouns that will be studied in this unit are the **personal** and **possessive pronouns**.

◆ The Personal Pronouns correspond to the three grammar persons.

First Person	Person speaking	*I, me, we, us*
Second Person	Person spoken to	*you*
Third Person	Person spoken about	*he, him, she, her, it, they, them*

◆ In this unit we will study only the 1st and 2nd person pronouns. Third person pronouns will be covered in *Third Form* with demonstrative pronouns.

◆ Pronouns can be confusing for three reasons:
1) pronouns have an attribute of verbs (*person*) and attributes of nouns (*case* and *gender*).
2) pronouns must agree with their antecedents.
3) some pronouns can also function as adjectives.

◆ Learn the **Pronoun Agreement Rule**: A pronoun agrees with its **antecedent** in gender and number, but its case is determined by its own clause.

◆ A prepositional phrase consists of a preposition, its object, and any modifiers. The preposition shows the relationship between its object and another word in the sentence.

◆ The object of a preposition is in either the ablative or accusative case. A dictionary entry for a preposition includes the case the preposition takes, or **governs**.

UNIT II

PERSONAL PRONOUNS

PREPOSITIONS

Pont du Gard

The **Pont du Gard** in southern France is one of the best preserved of the ancient Roman aqueduct bridges. Across the empire, Roman aqueducts carried clean water to Roman cities for homes, baths, and fountains. Like the Roman roads, they are marvels of Roman engineering and a testament to the practical genius of the Roman people. The construction methods are well described in **De Architectura**, written in the 1st century B.C. by Vitruvius. Most aqueducts were actually underground, and magnificent structures like the one above also served as bridges.

Ego sum via et véritas et vita.   *I am the way, the truth, and the life.*

First Person Pronouns

Case	S.	Meaning	Pl.	Meaning
nom.	**ego**	I	**nos**	we
gen.	**mei**	of me	**nostri, nostrum**[1]	of us
dat.	**mihi**	to/for me	**nobis**	to/for us
acc.	**me**	me	**nos**	us
abl.	**me**	in, by, with, from me	**nobis**	in, by, with, from us

♦   1st person pronouns have forms for number and case, but not gender.

Vocabulary

Latin	Gender	English	Derivative(s)
aqua -ae	*f.*	water	*aquarium*
culpa -ae	*f.*	fault, blame	*culprit*
ira -ae	*f.*	anger	*irate*
luna -ae	*f.*	moon	*lunatic*
silva -ae	*f.*	forest	*sylvan, Pennsylvania*
stella -ae	*f.*	star	*stellar*
umbra -ae	*f.*	shadow	*umbrella*
unda -ae	*f.*	wave	*undulate*
ursa -ae	*f.*	bear	*Ursa Major*
vita -ae	*f.*	life	*vitamin*

[1]**Nostri** is the objective genitive, *fear of us.* **Nostrum** is the partitive genitive, *part of us.*

◆ The nominative of the personal pronoun is used only for emphasis or contrast, since the verb ending is usually sufficient to indicate the person.

      Mariam amo. *I like Mary.*   **Ego Mariam amo.** *I like Mary.* (emphasizing *I!*)

◆ Notice that the nominative and accusative forms of *we* and *us* are different in English, but the same in Latin, **nos**.

◆ The genitive forms, **mei** and **nostri, nostrum**, are *not* used to show possession. They are used for other **of** expressions such as those indicated in the last bullet of Lesson V.

◆ **Silva** is often used in the plural to mean *forest* or *woods*.

> In John 14:6, Jesus tells the disciples that he will go to prepare a place for them, and when Thomas asks how they would know the way, Jesus responds, **"Ego sum via et véritas et vita."**

Oral Drill

1.	**silvam**	1.	we
2.	**nobis**	2.	us
3.	**stellis**	3.	of me
4.	**ego**	4.	to/for me
5.	**mihi**	5.	in/by/with/from me
6.	**undas**	6.	to/for us
7.	**mei**	7.	of us
8.	**nos**	8.	to/for the shadows
9.	**aquarum**	9.	I
10.	**me**	10.	me (d.o.)

Et tu, Brute? *You too, Brutus?*

Second Person Pronouns

Case	S.	Meaning	Pl.	Meaning
nom.	**tu**	you	**vos**	you all
gen.	**tui**	of you	**vestri, vestrum**[1]	of you all
dat.	**tibi**	to/for you	**vobis**	to/for you all
acc.	**te**	you	**vos**	you all
abl.	**te**	in, by, with, from you	**vobis**	in, by, with, from you all

♦ 1st and 2nd person pronouns have forms for number and case, but not gender.

Vocabulary

Latin	Gender	English	Derivative(s)
fília[2] **-ae**	*f.*	daughter	*filial*
Gállia -ae	*f.*	Gaul	*Gallic*
grátia -ae	*f.*	grace, favor, thanks (pl.)	*gracious*
Hispánia -ae	*f.*	Spain	*Hispanic*
Lúcia -ae	*f.*	Lucy	
pátria -ae	*f.*	fatherland, country	*patriotic*
pecúnia -ae	*f.*	money	
província -ae	*f.*	province	*provincial*
via -ae	*f.*	road, way	*viaduct*
victória -ae	*f.*	victory	*victorious*

[1] **Vestri** is the objective genitive. **Vestrum** is the partitive genitive.
[2] **Filia** is **filiabus** in the dative and ablative plural.

◆ The nominative of the personal pronoun is used only for emphasis or contrast, since the verb ending is usually sufficient to indicate the person.

| **Mariam amas.** | You like Mary. |
| **Ego Mariam amo, sed tu Lúciam amas.** | *I* love Mary, but *you* love Lucy. |

◆ The genitive forms **tui** and **vestri, vestrum** are *not* used to show possession. They are used for other **of** expressions such as those indicated in the last bullet of Lesson V.

Et tu, Brute? comes from Shakespeare's *Julius Caesar*. These are the words Caesar speaks as he is being assassinated. Brutus had been Caesar's young protégé during the Gallic campaigns, and Caesar was dismayed and shocked to find him among the assassins. **Et tu, Brute** is the classic expression of betrayal.

Oral Drill

1.	**tui**	1.	you all (sub.)
2.	**filiarum**	2.	you (d.o.)
3.	**vos**	3.	to/for you
4.	**vestrum**	4.	of you
5.	**Hispániam**	5.	ibwf you all
6.	**te**	6.	ibwf you
7.	**vobis**	7.	you all (d.o.)
8.	**vestri**	8.	you (sub.)
9.	**tu**	9.	of you all
10.	**tibi**	10.	to/for you all

mea culpa *my fault*

1st/2nd Person Possessive Pronoun Adjectives

Person	S.	Meaning	Pl.	Meaning
1	**meus mea meum**	my	**noster, nostra, nostrum**	our
2	**tuus tua tuum**	your	**vester, vestra, vestrum**	your *(pl.)*

♦ **Meus, tuus, noster,** and **vester** are used to show possession for 1st and 2nd person pronouns. They function as regular 1st/2nd declension adjectives. An adjective agrees with its noun in gender, number, and case.

> **mea mensa** *my table*   **meas mensas** *my tables (acc.)*   **meus frater** *my brother*

♦ A noun has to be in the genitive case to be possessive. **Meus, tuus, noster,** and **vester** are possessive <u>by definition</u>. They can be written in <u>all</u> cases, not just the genitive case.

Vocabulary

Latin	Gender	English	Derivative(s)
áquila -ae	*f.*	eagle	*aquiline*
aurora -ae	*f.*	dawn	*aurora borealis*
corona -ae	*f.*	crown	*coronation*
culina -ae	*f.*	kitchen	*culinary*
fábula -ae	*f.*	story, tale	*fabulous*
fémina -ae	*f.*	woman	*feminine*
fenestra -ae	*f.*	window	
fortuna -ae	*f.*	fortune	*fortunate*
ínsula -ae	*f.*	island	*insulate*
jánua -ae	*f.*	door	*January*

♦ **Meus, tuus, noster,** and **vester** are also pronouns. There is an understood **antecedent**, which is either singular or plural, and male, female, or neuter.

♦ There are two nouns involved with every form of **meus, tuus, noster,** and **vester**: the noun modified and the understood antecedent. Remember these words function as adjectives and obey the adjective agreement rule, <u>not</u> the pronoun agreement rule. They agree in gender, number, and case with the nouns they modify, not with their antecedents.

1) For **meus** and **tuus** the understood antecedent is singular, *I* and *you,* but the noun modified may be singular <u>or</u> plural.

mea mensa	*my table*	**meae mensae**	*my tables*

2) **Mea mensa** is feminine because the table is feminine, not the understood antecedent.
Meus servus is masculine because the servant is masculine, not the understood antecedent.

> **Mea culpa** comes from the confiteor of the Latin Mass in which the faithful would say, **mea culpa, mea culpa, mea maxima culpa.** *Through my fault, through my fault, through my most grievous fault.* **Mea culpa** is a very common Latin expression, used especially by public figures who want to acknowledge a mistake.

Janus

Usually portrayed with two faces, one facing the future, the other the past, Janus was the god of gates, doors, beginnings, and endings. He has given his name to January, the first month of the year.

Ab Urbe Cónditā   *From the founding of the city*

Prepositions with Ablative

Latin	English	Derivatives
a, ab	by, from	*absent*
coram	in the presence of	
cum	with	*contact, compact*
de	about, down from	*devalue*
e, ex	out of, out from	*exclude*
in	in, on	*include*
prae	at the head of	*predict*
pro	for, on behalf of, in front of	*prologue*
sine	without	*sinecure*
sub	under, at the foot of	*subway*
tenus	as far as	

Vocabulary

Latin	Gender	English	Derivative(s)
ara -ae	*f.*	altar	
epístula -ae	*f.*	letter	*epistle*
porta -ae	*f.*	gate	*portal*
sella -ae	*f.*	seat	
villa -ae	*f.*	farmhouse	*villa*

♦ A preposition shows the relationship between a noun/pronoun and another word in the sentence.

♦ A prepositional phrase consists of the preposition and its object[1]. In Latin the object is in either the ablative or accusative case. The prepositions in this lesson *govern*, or take, the ablative.

sine amico	without a friend	**sine nobis**	without us

♦ The prepositions **ab** and **ex** have shortened forms, **a** and **e**, before words beginning with consonants, in a manner similar to the articles *a* and *an* in English.

♦ **Cum** is added to the end of the ablative forms of 1st and 2nd person pronouns, **me, nobis, te, vobis,** to create one word.

mecum	with me	**nobiscum**	with us
tecum	with you	**vobiscum**	with you all

♦ **Dominus vobiscum,** *The Lord be with you*, is a common expression in Christian Latin.

♦ You can learn these prepositions that take the ablative in order to the tune of *O Christmas Tree*.

♦ Note: Many Latin prepositions are translated by compound prepositions of two or more words in English. Many of these compound prepositions in English end in **of**. Do not be confused and put the object of the preposition in the genitive case when you see the word **of** at the end of a compound preposition.

> *Ab Urbe Conditā* is the title of Livy's monumental history of Rome from the founding of the city until the reign of Augustus. Titius Livius was born in Padua in 59 B.C. and apparently spent his whole life writing his history, originally consisting of 142 books, of which 32 survive. Livy's fascinating and entertaining narrative has a clear message—Rome was destined by the gods to be the conqueror and ruler of the nations.

[1] The object may have modifiers.

Hánnibal ad portas *Hannibal at the gates*

Prepositions with Accusative

Latin	English	Derivative(s)
ad	to, toward, at	*adventure*
ante	before (in time and place)	*antecedent*
apud	among	
in	into, onto	*inspect*
inter	between	*interstellar*
ob	because of	*object*
per	through	*persist*
post	after, behind	*post meridian, P.M.*
propter	on account of	
sub	to the foot of	*subway*
trans	across	*transport*
circum	around	*circumvent*
contra	against	*contradict*
juxta	near	*juxtapose*

Vocabulary

Latin	Gender	English	Derivative(s)
cena -ae	*f.*	dinner	
herba -ae	*f.*	green plant, grass	*herb*
tabella -ae	*f.*	writing tablet	
turba -ae	*f.*	crowd, turmoil	*turbulent*
vacca -ae	*f.*	cow	*vaccine*

- The p

- You c
  Baby L

- Genera
  express

- The prep

[Note card overlapping text:]

Song:
ad ante apud
in inter ob
per post propter
sub et trans
~~Latin prepositions,~~ circum et contra
~~learn them all with ease.~~ juxta quoque
Latin prepositions,
take accusative.

...ve to the tune of *Mama's Little*

...usative, and prepositions which

...ablative.

Latin	With Accusative indicates motion	With Ablative indicates location
in	into, onto	in, on
sub	to (up to) the foot of	under, at the foot of

in with the ablative Lucius <u>in agro</u> stat. Luke stands in the field.

in with the accusative Lucius <u>in agrum</u> ambulat. Luke walks into the field.

> **Hánnibal ad portas** was a proverbial threat of impending calamity, referring to the time immediately after Rome's disastrous defeat by Hannibal at Cannae, when Hannibal brought his army right up to the walls and gates of Rome.

Hannibal

This statue, found at Capua, is thought to be an image of Hannibal, the Carthaginian general who led his army and elephants across the Alps to invade Italy and destroy Rome. After Rome suffered massive defeats in four pitched battles with Hannibal, she realized she was in a life and death struggle with one of the greatest generals of all time. The perseverance and patience of Rome, however, eventually overcame the genius of Hannibal, and the confidence Rome gained from her extraordinary struggle with Carthage prepared her for her ultimate destiny.

Personal Pronouns

Case	First Person		Second Person	
	S.	Pl.	S.	Pl.
nom.	ego	nos	tu	vos
gen.	mei	nostri, nostrum	tui	vestri, vestrum
dat.	mihi	nobis	tibi	vobis
acc.	me	nos	te	vos
abl.	me	nobis	te	vobis

Prepositions

with ablative		with accusative	
a, ab	by, from	**ad**	to, toward, at
coram	in the presence of	**ante**	before (in time and place)
cum	with	**apud**	among
de	about, down from	**in**	into, onto
e, ex	out of, out from	**inter**	between
in	in, on	**ob**	because of
prae	at the head of	**per**	through
pro	for, on behalf of, in front of	**post**	after, behind
sine	without	**propter**	on account of
sub	under, at the foot of	**sub**	to the foot of
tenus	as far as	**trans**	across
		circum	around
		contra	against
		juxta	near

Vocabulary Review

áquila -ae	f.	eagle		luna -ae	f.	moon
aqua -ae	f.	water		pátria -ae	f.	fatherland, country
ara -ae	f.	altar		pecúnia -ae	f.	money
aurora -ae	f.	dawn		porta -ae	f.	gate
cena -ae	f.	dinner		província -ae	f.	province
corona -ae	f.	crown		sella -ae	f.	seat
culina -ae	f.	kitchen		stella -ae	f.	star
culpa -ae	f.	fault, blame		silva -ae	f.	forest
epístula -ae	f.	letter		tabella -ae	f.	writing tablet
fábula -ae	f.	story, tale		turba -ae	f.	crowd, turmoil
fémina -ae	f.	woman		umbra -ae	f.	shadow
fenestra -ae	f.	window		unda -ae	f.	wave
fília -ae	f.	daughter		ursa -ae	f.	bear
fortuna -ae	f.	fortune		vacca -ae	f.	cow
Gállia -ae	f.	Gaul		via -ae	f.	way, road
grátia -ae	f.	grace, favor, thanks (pl)		victória -ae	f.	victory
herba -ae	f.	green plant, grass		villa -ae	f.	farmhouse
Hispánia -ae	f.	Spain		vita -ae	f.	life
ínsula -ae	f.	island		meus -a -um		my
ira -ae	f.	anger		tuus -a -um		your
jánua -ae	f.	door		noster nostra nostrum		our
Lúcia -ae	f.	Lucy		vester vestra vestrum		your (pl.)

Grammar Review

♦ **Pronoun Agreement Rule:** A pronoun agrees with its antecedent in gender and number, but its case is determined by its own clause.

♦ 1st/2nd Person Possessive Pronoun Adjectives, **meus, tuus, noster,** and **vester,** function as regular 1st/2nd declension adjectives.

♦ Prepositions govern either the ablative or accusative cases. Two prepositions, **in** and **sub,** can govern either case.

Latin Sayings

Ego Sum Via et Véritas et Vita

mea culpa

Hánnibal ad portas

Et tu, Brute?

Ab Urbe Cóndita

◆ In the first lesson of this unit, Lesson XIV, you will review:
  1) the Present System of the 1st and 2nd conjugations and the irregular verb **sum**
  2) the first two principal parts of the fifty 1st conj. and twenty 2nd conj. *First Form* verbs

◆ Then you will learn the Present System of the 3rd and 4th conjugations. The 3rd and 4th conjugations are learned together because they are very similar.

◆ The 3rd and 4th conjugations have the same personal endings **(o, s, t, mus, tis, nt)** as 1st and 2nd conjugation verbs, but different tense signs in the present and future tenses.

◆ The 3rd conjugation has a subgroup called **io** verbs. Fortunately, the Present System of the **io** verbs is the same as that of the 3rd and 4th conjugations.

◆ You will learn the first two principal parts of twenty-five 3rd and 4th conjugation verbs.

◆ The infinitive ending of the 3rd conjugation is **ere**, which is not to be confused with the **ēre** ending of the 2nd conjugation infinitive.

◆ The infinitive ending of the 4th conjugation is **ire**.

◆ An adverb modifies a verb, adjective, or another adverb. Adverbs answer the questions *how, when, where, to what extent.*

◆ Many 1st/2nd declension adjectives can be changed into adverbs by adding **ē** to the stem.

◆ Many 3rd declension adjectives can be changed into adverbs by adding **iter** to the stem.

Antonine Wall

Construction of another wall at the Firth of Forth and the Firth of Clyde in Scotland was begun during the reign of the emperor Antonius Pius, in A.D. 142. But the Romans withdrew back to Hadrian's Wall after only twenty years. There are few remains of the Antonine Wall.

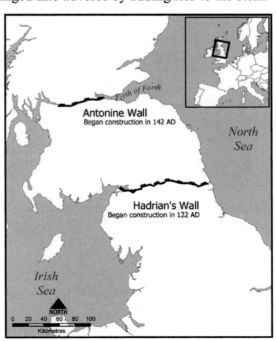

Antonine Wall
Began construction in 142 AD

North Sea

Firth of Forth

Hadrian's Wall
Began construction in 122 AD

Irish Sea

NORTH

0 20 40 60 80 100
Kilometres

UNIT III

VERBS

3RD AND 4TH CONJUGATIONS INDICATIVE ACTIVE PRESENT SYSTEM

Hadrian's Wall

Begun by the emperor Hadrian in A.D. 122, this stone and wood fortification across northern Britain was effectively the northern border of the Empire. It reflected the shift in Roman policy from expansion to consolidation. Originally much higher than what you see here and punctuated by towers and army camps, the wall was as much a means of contact as a barrier, where commerce took place between Roman soldiers and native Celts to the north.

First Form Review

Ist and 2nd Conjugations and **Sum** - Present System

	Present		Imperfect		Future	
	S.	Pl.	S.	Pl.	S.	Pl.
1st Conj.	amo	amamus	amabam	amabamus	amabo	amábimus
	amas	amatis	amabas	amabatis	amabis	amábitis
	amat	amant	amabat	amabant	amabit	amabunt
2nd Conj.	móneo	monemus	monebam	monebamus	monebo	monébimis
	mones	monetis	monebas	monebatis	monebis	monébitis
	monet	monent	monebat	monebant	monebit	monebunt
Sum	sum	sumus	eram	eramus	ero	érimus
	es	estis	eras	eratis	eris	éritis
	est	sunt	erat	erant	erit	erunt

Latin Sayings

In choro recitemus

Civis Romanus sum.

Stabat Mater

In umbra, ígitur, pugnábimus.

Vídeo et táceo.

Cave canem.

Docēre, delectare, movēre

Adverbs

heri	*yesterday*	**nunc**	*now*
hódie	*today*	**saepe**	*often*
cras	*tomorrow*	**semper**	*always*
non	*not*	**tum**	*then, at that time*
numquam	*never*	**umquam**	*ever*

♦ The translations for the present system, indicative active, of 1st and 2nd conjugation verbs and **sum,** are in the appendix, p. 102. There are three translations for the present tense: the *simple* present, *progressive* present, and *emphatic* present. The imperfect tense describes an ongoing action in the past and is translated by the English helping verbs *was* and *were*. The future tense is translated with the helping verb *will*.

♦ The present system is built on the present stem, which for 1st/2nd conjugation verbs, is found by dropping the **re** from the 2nd principal part, the **infinitive.** The infinitive of 1st conjugation verbs ends in **are;** for 2nd conjugation verbs, **ēre**. The stem vowel of the 1st conjugation is **a,** and of the 2nd, **e**.

accuso (1) to accuse
adoro (1) to adore
ámbulo (1) to walk
amo (1) to love, like
appáreo (2) to appear
appello (1) to address
árdeo ardēre to burn, be on fire
aro (1) to plow
cáveo cavēre to beware of, guard against
celo (1) to hide
clamo (1) to shout
creo (1) to create
culpo (1) to blame
débeo (2) to owe, ought
delecto (1) to delight, please
demonstro (1) to show, point out
do dare to give
dóceo docēre to teach
dúbito (1) to doubt
erro (1) to err, wander
exploro (1) to explore
exspecto (1) to wait for, expect
gáudeo gaudēre to rejoice
hábeo (2) to have
hábito (1) to live in, dwell
júbeo jubēre to order
júdico (1) to judge, consider
juvo juvare to help
laboro (1) to work
laudo (1) to praise
lavo lavare lto wash
líbero (1) to free, set free
máneo manēre to remain, stay
móneo (2) to warn
móveo movēre to move
muto (1) to change

narro (1) to tell
nato (1) to swim
návigo (1) to sail
nego (1) to deny
núntio (1) to report
óccupo (1) to seize
oppugno (1) to attack
opto (1) to desire, wish
oro (1) to speak, pray
paro (1) to prepare
perturbo (1) to disturb
porto (1) to carry
prohíbeo (2) to prevent
pugno (1) to fight
puto (1) to think
respóndeo -spondēre to respond
rogo (1) to ask
saluto (1) to greet
sédeo sedēre to sit
servo (1) to guard, keep
specto (1) to look at
spero (1) to hope
sto stare to stand
súpero (1) to overcome
táceo (2) to be silent
tempto (1) to tempt
téneo tenēre to hold
térreo (2) to frighten
tímeo timēre to fear, be afraid of
váleo valēre to be strong, be well
vídeo vidēre to see
voco (1) to call
volo (1) to fly
vúlnero (1) to wound

sum esse to be

In hoc signo vinces. *In this sign you will conquer.*

Present System 3rd Conjugation

rego régere I rule present stem: **reg-**

Person	Present		Imperfect		Future	
	S.	Pl.	S.	Pl.	S.	Pl.
1	*reg*o	*rég*imus	*reg*ebam	*reg*ebamus	*reg*am	*reg*emus
2	*reg*is	*rég*itis	*reg*ebas	*reg*ebatis	*reg*es	*reg*etis
3	*reg*it	*reg*unt	*reg*ebat	*reg*ebant	*reg*et	*reg*ent

◆ The infinitive ending for 3rd conjugation verbs is **ere**. The infinitive ending for 2nd conjugation verbs is **ēre**. The first **e** of the infinitive is a long **ē** in the 2nd conjugation, and a short **e** in the 3rd.

◆ Study the present system of the 3rd conjugation model verb **rego**. The 3rd conjugation does not follow the clear consistent patterns of the 1st and 2nd conjugations. Dropping the **re** from the infinitive does not give a stem with a consistent stem vowel.

◆ To form the present system of a 3rd conjugation verb, the **root** without a stem vowel must serve as the stem. To find the **root**, drop the whole infinitive ending from the 2nd principal part.

1st p.p.	*2nd p.p.*	*root (stem)*
rego	**reg/ere**	**reg**

Vocabulary

Latin	English	Derivative(s)
dico dícere	to say, tell	*dictator, dictation*
duco dúcere	to lead	*duct*
figo fígere	to fix, fasten	*fixation*
jungo júngere	to join, connect	*junction*
rego régere	to rule	*direct*
struo strúere	to build, construct	*structure*
traho tráhere	to drag, haul	*traction, tractor*
veho véhere	to convey, transport	*vehicle*
vivo vívere	to live, be alive	*vivid*
vinco víncere	to conquer	*invincible*

♦ Learn these endings to form the present tense: **o, is, it, imus, itis, unt**. The personal endings are regular, but the vowel changes. **Tip:** remember **IOU**. (I in four forms, U in the last, and O in the first) **Tip:** These endings are identical to the 1st/2nd conj. future endings without the letter **b**.

♦ The imperfect tense is regular, just what you would expect it to be. Learn these endings to form the imperfect tense: **ebam, ebas, ebat, ebamus, ebatis, ebant**.

♦ Learn these endings to form the future tense: **am, es, et, emus, etis, ent**. Again the personal endings are regular, but the vowel changes. **Tip:** remember **AE**. (A in the first form and E in the other five forms)

♦ All five vowels **AE/IOU** are represented in the present system, rather than one consistent stem vowel.

♦ One more tip for remembering the future tense: Why is the 3rd conjugation an old maid? Because it has no **bo's** in its future!

♦ The present system of the 3rd conjugation is perhaps the most difficult paradigm students encounter in Latin, not because it is inherently difficult, but because it is so unexpected and irregular compared to the beautiful consistency of the first two conjugations.

The Arch of Constantine

The Arch of Constantine, a triumphal arch situated between the Colosseum and the Palatine Hill, was built to commemorate Constantine's victory over Maxentius in the battle of Milvian Bridge.

In hoc signo vinces. Before the Battle of Milvian Bridge on October 28, A.D. 312, Constantine saw a vision of a cross in the sky inscribed with these words. After marking the shields of his soldiers with the sign of the cross, Constantine defeated Maxentius, and became sole emperor of the Roman Empire. Constantine attributed his victory to the protection of the Christian God and changed the course of world history when he ended the persecutions of his predecessor, Diocletian, legalized Christianity, and became the first Christian Emperor.

Aut viam invéniam aut fáciam.   *I shall either find a way or make one.*

Present System 4th Conjugation

áudio audíre   I hear   present stem: **audí-**

	Present		Imperfect		Future	
	S.	Pl.	S.	Pl.	S.	Pl.
1	*áudi* o	*audi* mus	*audi* ebam	*audi* ebamus	*áudi* am	*audi* emus
2	*audi* s	*audi* tis	*audi* ebas	*audi* ebatis	*áudi* es	*audi* etis
3	*audi* t	*áudi* unt	*audi* ebat	*audi* ebant	*áudi* et	*áudi* ent

♦ The infinitive ending for the 4th conjugation is **ire**. Dropping the **re** from the infinitive gives a consistent stem for the 4th conjugation.

audio   audire   audi / re   =   audi

♦ The present system of the 4th conjugation is essentially the same as the 3rd conjugation with the addition of the stem vowel **i**.

Vocabulary

Latin	English	Derivative(s)
áudio audire	to hear	*audition, audio*
dórmio dormire	to sleep	*dormitory*
fínio finire	to finish, limit	*finish, finite*
impédio impedire	to hinder, obstruct	*impede*
invénio invenire	to discover, find out	*invent*
múnio munire	to fortify, protect	*ammunition*
néscio nescire	to not know	
séntio sentire	to feel, perceive	*sensitive*
scio scire	to know	*science*
vénio venire	to come	*advent*

◆ The present tense endings are: **o, s, t, mus, tis, unt**. The imperfect tense endings are: **ebam, ebas, ebat, ebamus, ebatis, ebant**. The future tense the endings are: **am, es, et, emus, etis, ent**.

◆ All five vowels **AE/IOU** are represented in the Present System, and like the 3rd conjugation the 4th is an old maid because it has no **bo's** in its future.

◆ Even though the irregularity of the 3rd conjugation present system is disappointing, be consoled by these considerations: 1) The personal endings are entirely regular. 2) The imperfect tense is entirely regular. 3) The 4th conjugation is very similar to the 3rd, so once this lesson is mastered the next will present no problems. 4) The perfect system, as well as all other forms of the Latin verb system, maintain the beautiful regularity you have come to expect from Latin verbs.

> **Aut viam invéniam aut fáciam** is a favorite motto of enterprising individuals. Its origins are obscure. We express the same idea with the expression, *Where there's a will there's a way.*

Form Drill

1.	muniebamus	1.	I will finish
2.	sciam	2.	they were obstructing
3.	dórmiunt	3.	you know
4.	impédiet	4.	we were finishing
5.	audis	5.	they were protecting
6.	nesciebam	6.	you all will come
7.	finiemus	7.	he does not know
8.	munit	8.	she will sleep
9.	veniebatis	9.	he was hearing
10.	áudies	10.	we protect

45

Tempus fugit   *Time flies*

Present System

3rd Conjugation **io** Verbs

cápio capere   I take   present stem: **capi-**

Present		Imperfect		Future	
S.	Pl.	S.	Pl.	S.	Pl.
1	*cápi**o***	*cápi**mus***	*capi**ebam***	*capi**ebamus***	*cápi**am***	*capi**emus***
2	*capi**s***	*cápi**tis***	*capi**ebas***	*capi**ebatis***	*cápi**es***	*capi**etis***
3	*capi**t***	*cápi**unt***	*capi**ebat***	*capi**ebant***	*cápi**et***	*cápi**ent***

◆ Study the entry form, the infinitive, and the conjugation of these five verbs.

◆ These verbs are called **io** verbs of the 3rd conjugation. They are 3rd conjugation because the infinitive ending is **ere**, but the entry form and present system look identical to the 4th conjugation.

◆ To form the present system of **io** verbs of the 3rd conjugation, find the stem from the entry form and add the endings of the 4th conjugation.

capio   capere   **capi /o = capi**

Vocabulary

Latin		English	Derivative
cápio	**cápere**	to take, capture	*capture*
cúpio	**cúpere**	to desire, wish for	*cupid*
fácio	**fácere**	to make, do	*fact*
fúgio	**fúgere**	to flee	*fugitive*
jácio	**jácere**	to throw	*eject*

Tempus fugit is taken from the third book of Vergil's *Georgics*. It often appears on clocks and expresses a truth we all know from experience.

Relief from Ara Pacis

The Ara Pacis of Augustus, commissioned by the Senate in 4 B.C., is an Altar to Peace, celebrating the end of the Civil Wars and the beginning of what came to be know as the Pax Romana. This panel depicts Mother Earth, Tellus, with twins, the Roman people, and a cow, sheep, and wheat symbolizing the bounty of the land in times of peace.

Oral Drill

1.	faciemus	1.	they make
2.	jacit	2.	I was desiring
3.	cápiunt	3.	you throw
4.	cupiebas	4.	they will capture
5.	jácient	5.	you all were fleeing
6.	fúgitis	6.	they wish for
7.	fáciam	7.	I make
8.	cupiebant	8.	she was fleeing
9.	capis	9.	it will capture
10.	faciebamus	10.	we desire

Festina lentē *Make haste slowly*

1st/2nd Declension Adjectives and Adverbs

Adjective	Meaning	Adverb	Meaning
altus -a -um	high, deep	altē	highly, deeply
latus -a -um	wide, broad	latē	widely
liber -a -um	free	líberē	freely
pulcher pulchra pulchrum	beautiful	pulchrē	beautifully
asper -a -um	sharp, harsh	ásperē	roughly
miser -a -um	wretched	míserē	unhappily
multus -a -um	much, many	multum	much

New Vocabulary			
longus -a -um	long	longē	far, by far
laetus -a -um	happy	laetē	happily
lentus -a -um	slow	lentē	slowly
certus -a -um	certain	certē	certainly

3rd Declension Adjectives and Adverbs

Adjective	Meaning	Adverb	Meaning
brévis -e	short, brief	brév iter	shortly, briefly
gravis -e	heavy	gráv iter	heavily, seriously
fortis -e	strong, brave	fórt iter	bravely
fidelis -e	faithful	fidél iter	faithfully
difficilis -e	difficult	difficíl iter	with difficulty
turpis -e	shameful, disgraceful	túrp iter	shamefully
fácilis -e	easy	fácile	easily

♦ An adverb is a word that modifies a verb, adjective, or another adverb.

♦ Most often an adverb modifies a verb and answers the questions *how, when, where, to what extent.*

♦ In English we often add **ly** to an adjective to change it to an adverb.

♦ In Latin a large number of adverbs are also formed from adjectives. Many adverbs are formed from 1st/2nd declension adjectives by adding an **ē** to the adj. stem.

adjective	*meaning*	*adverb*	*meaning*
latus, a, um	wide	**latē**	widely
liber, líbera, líberum	free	**liberē**	freely

♦ Many adverbs are formed from 3rd declension adjectives by adding **iter** to the adj. stem.

adjective	*meaning*	*adverb*	*meaning*
brevis -e	short, brief	**breviter**	shortly, briefly

♦ Some adjectives use the neuter singular accusative form as an adverb.

In 1st/2nd declension adjectives, the neuter singular accusative form ends in **um**.

adjective	*meaning*	*adverb*	*meaning*
multus -a -um	much, many	**multum**	much

In 3rd declension adjectives, the neuter singular accusative form ends in **e** (no macron over the **e**).

adjective	*meaning*	*adverb*	*meaning*
facilis -e	easy	**facile**	easily

> **Festina lentē** is attributed to Augustus Caesar. It expresses the idea of accomplishing much, but in slow careful steps.

3rd, 4th and 3rd *io* Conjugations - Present System

Tense	Number	3rd Conj.	4th Conj.	3rd **io** Conj.
Present	sing.	*reg*o *reg*is *reg*it	*áudi*o *audi*s *audi*t	*cápi*o *capi*s *capi*t
	pl.	*rég*imus *rég*itis *reg*unt	*audi*mus *audi*tis *áudi*unt	*cápi*mus *cápi*tis *cápi*unt
Imperfect	sing.	*reg*ebam *reg*ebas *reg*ebat	*audi*ebam *audi*ebas *audi*ebat	*capi*ebam *capi*ebas *capi*ebat
	pl.	*reg*ebamus *reg*ebatis *reg*ebant	*audi*ebamus *audi*ebatis *audi*ebant	*capi*ebamus *capi*ebatis *capi*ebant
Future	sing.	*reg*am *reg*es *reg*et	*áudi*am *áudi*es *áudi*et	*cápi*am *cápi*es *cápi*et
	pl.	*reg*emus *reg*etis *reg*ent	*audi*emus *audi*etis *áudi*ent	*capi*emus *capi*etis *cápi*ent

Latin Sayings

In hoc signo vinces.
Tempus fugit

Aut viam invéniam aut fáciam.
Festina lentē

Vocabulary Review - Verbs

áudio audire	to hear		**jungo júngere**	to join, connect
cápio cápere	to take, capture		**múnio munire**	to fortify, protect
cúpio cúpere	to desire, wish for		**néscio nescire**	to not know
dico dícere	to say, tell		**rego régere**	to rule
dórmio dormire	to sleep		**scio scire**	to know
duco dúcere	to lead		**séntio sentire**	to feel, perceive
fácio fácere	to make, do		**struo strúere**	to build, construct
figo fígere	to fix, fasten		**traho tráhere**	to drag, haul
fínio finire	to finish, limit		**veho véhere**	to carry, convey, transport
fúgio fúgere	to flee		**vénio venire**	to come
impédio impedire	to hinder, obstruct		**vinco víncere**	to conquer
invénio invenire	to discover, find out		**vivo vívere**	to live, be alive
jácio jácere	to throw			

Vocabulary Review - Adjectives and Adverbs

altē	highly, deeply		**laetus -a -um**	happy
ásperē	roughly		**latē**	widely
bréviter	shortly, briefly		**lentē**	slowly
certē	certainly		**lentus -a -um**	slow
certus -a -um	certain		**líberē**	freely
difficíliter	with difficulty		**longē**	far, by far
fácile	easily		**longus -a -um**	long
fidéliter	faithfully		**míserē**	unhappily
fórtiter	bravely		**multum**	much
gráviter	heavily		**pulchrē**	beautifully
laetē	happily		**túrpiter**	shamefully

♦ In the first lesson of this unit you will review:
   1) the Perfect System of the 1st and 2nd conjugations, and the irregular verb **sum**
   2) all principal parts of the fifty 1st conj. and twenty 2nd conj. *First Form* verbs

♦ In this unit you will learn the Perfect System of the 3rd, 4th, and 3rd **io** conjugations.

♦ The Perfect System of 3rd, 4th, and 3rd **io** conjugations is identical to the Perfect System of the 1st and 2nd conjugations. The Perfect System of all four conjugations is perfectly regular.

♦ 3rd conjugation verbs do <u>not</u> have one model for regular principal parts. The principal parts of 3rd conjugation verbs will be learned in pattern groups. The first pattern you will learn follows the model verb **rego**.

♦ 4th conjugation verbs <u>do</u> have regular principal parts that follow the model verb **audio**.

♦ There are two kinds of direct questions in Latin and English:
   1) yes or no questions
   2) questions that begin with interrogative words

Trajan's Column Reliefs

UNIT IV

Verbs

3rd & 4th Conjugations
Indicative Active
Perfect System

Trajan's Column

Trajan's Column, built to commemorate Trajan's victory over the Dacians, depicts scenes from the Dacian war in a continuous spiral. The column, once topped with a statue of Trajan, is now topped with a statue of St. Peter.

First Form Review

1st and 2nd Conjugations and **Sum** - Perfect System

	Perfect		Pluperfect		Future Perfect	
	S.	Pl.	S.	Pl.	S.	Pl.
1st Conj.	amavi	amávimus	amáveram	amaveramus	amávero	amavérimus
	amavisti	amavistis	amáveras	amaveratis	amáveris	amavéritis
	amavit	amaverunt	amáverat	amáverant	amáverit	amáverint
2nd Conj.	mónui	monúimus	monúeram	monueramus	monúero	monuérimus
	monuisti	monuistis	monúeras	monueratis	monúeris	monuéritis
	mónuit	monuerunt	monúerat	monúerant	monúerit	monúerint
Sum	fui	fúimus	fúeram	fueramus	fúero	fúerimus
	fuisti	fuistis	fúeras	fueratis	fúeris	fúeritis
	fuit	fuerunt	fúerat	fúerant	fúerit	fúerint

Latin Sayings

Errare est humanum.
Semper fidelis
Ora et labora.

Nunc aut numquam
Fortes fortuna juvat.
Veni, vidi, vici.

◆ The translations for the perfect system, indicative active, of 1st and 2nd conjugation verbs and **sum,** are in the appendix, p. 102. There are three English translations for the perfect tense:

	helping verbs	
the *simple* past	none	*I praised*
the *present* perfect	*have, has*	*I have praised*
the *emphatic* past	*did*	*I did praise*

◆ The English helping verb for the pluperfect tense is *had*, and for the future perfect tense, *will have*.

◆ The present system is built on the present stem. The perfect system is built on the perfect stem, which is found by dropping the **i** from the 3rd principal part.

amo   amare   amavi   amatus

accuso (1) to accuse
adoro (1) to adore
ámbulo (1) to walk
amo (1) to love, like
appáreo (2) to appear
appello (1) to address
árdeo ardēre arsi arsus to burn, be on fire
cáveo cavēre cavi cautus to beware of, guard against
celo (1) to hide
clamo (1) to shout
creo (1) to create
culpo (1) to blame
débeo (2) to owe, ought
delecto (1) to delight, please
demonstro (1) to show, point out
do dare dedi datus to give
dóceo docēre dócui doctus to teach
dúbito (1) to doubt
erro (1) to err, wander
exploro (1) to explore
exspecto (1) to wait for, expect
gáudeo gaudēre — — to rejoice
hábeo (2) to have
hábito (1) to live in, dwell
júbeo jubēre jussi jussus to order
júdico (1) to judge, consider
juvo juvare juvi jutus to help
laboro (1) to work
laudo (1) to praise
lavo lavare lavi lautus to wash
líbero (1) to set free
máneo manēre mansi mansus to remain, stay
móneo (2) to warn
móveo movēre movi motus to move
muto (1) to change

narro (1) to tell
nato (1) to swim
návigo (1) to sail
nego (1) to deny
núntio (1) to report
óccupo (1) to seize
oppugno (1) to attack
opto (1) to desire, wish
oro (1) to speak, pray
paro (1) to prepare
perturbo (1) to disturb
porto (1) to carry
prohíbeo (2) to prevent
pugno (1) to fight
puto (1) to think
respóndeo -spondēre -spondi -sponsus to respond
rogo (1) to ask
saluto (1) to greet
sédeo sedēre sedi sessus to sit
servo (1) to guard, keep
specto (1) to look at
spero (1) to hope
sto stare steti status to stand
súpero (1) to overcome
táceo (2) to be silent
tempto (1) to tempt
téneo tenēre ténui tentus to hold
térreo (2) to frighten
tímeo timēre tímui to fear, be afraid of
váleo valēre válui to be strong, be well
vídeo vidēre vidi visus to see
voco (1) to call
volo (1) to fly
vúlnero (1) to wound

sum esse fui futurus to be

Magister dixit. *The master has spoken.*

3rd Conjugation Perfect System

rego régere to rule *perfect stem* **rex-**

Perfect		Pluperfect		Future Perfect	
S.	Pl.	S.	Pl.	S.	Pl.
rex **i**	*réx* **imus**	*réx* **eram**	*rex* **eramus**	*réx* **ero**	*rex* **érimus**
rex **isti**	*rex* **istis**	*réx* **eras**	*rex* **eratis**	*réx* **eris**	*rex* **éritis**
rex **it**	*rex* **erunt**	*réx* **erat**	*réx* **erant**	*réx* **erit**	*réx* **erint**

◆ All verbs whose infinitive ends in **ere** belong to the 3rd conjugation. Notice there is no macron over the **e**. The first **e** is long in the 2nd conjugation, **ēre**, and short in the 3rd conjugation, **ere**.

◆ There are no regular endings for 3rd conjugation principal parts, but there are several patterns that are helpful. All verbs in this lesson, except for **vinco**, follow the pattern of **rego**.

Vocabulary

1st	2nd	3rd	4th	Meaning
rego	**régere**	**rexi**	**rectus**	to rule
dico	**dícere**	**dixi**	**dictus**	to say, speak, tell
duco	**dúcere**	**duxi**	**ductus**	to lead
figo	**figere**	**fixi**	**fictus**	to fix, fasten
jungo	**júngere**	**junxi**	**junctus**	to join, connect
struo	**strúere**	**struxi**	**structus**	to build, construct
traho	**tráhere**	**traxi**	**tractus**	to drag, haul
veho	**véhere**	**vexi**	**vectus**	to convey, transport
vivo	**vívere**	**vixi**	**victus** *(victum)*	to live, be alive
vinco	**vincere**	**vici**	**victus**	to conquer

Rego pattern - principal parts

1st	2nd	3rd	4th
rego	*régere*	*rexi*	*rectus*
I rule	to rule	I ruled	ruled
o	**ere**	**xi**	**ctus**

◆ The last consonant of the stem changes to **x** in the third principal part, and to **ct** in the fourth principal part. Note: The stem of **struo** ends in a vowel.

◆ To find the perfect stem, drop the personal ending **i** from the third principal part.

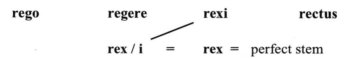

rego   regere   rexi   rectus

rex / i   =   rex = perfect stem

◆ The perfect system is perfectly regular in all four conjugations. The perfect system endings are the same as those you learned for the 1st/2nd conjugations.

> **Magister dixit** is a phrase whose origins lie in medieval school-ing, where the master was the ultimate authority. It also refers to the philosopher, Aristotle, the ultimate authority in all matters of natural reason in the medieval school.

Oral Drill

1.	**fíxerat**	1.	they had led
2.	**strúero**	2.	we will have said
3.	**vexisti**	3.	you all have conquered
4.	**vicit**	4.	she had built
5.	**júnxerint**	5.	they have hauled
6.	**dixerunt**	6.	we had conveyed
7.	**dúxeram**	7.	I will have joined
8.	**rexérimus**	8.	you had fastened
9.	**vixi**	9.	it has ruled
10.	**traxeramus**	10.	he had led

A mari usque ad mare   *From sea to sea*

4th Conjugation   Perfect System

áudio audíre   to hear   *perfect stem* **audiv-**

	Perfect			Pluperfect			Future Perfect	
	S.	Pl.		S.	Pl.		S.	Pl.
1	*audiv*i	*audív*imus		*audív*eram	*audív*eramus		*audív*ero	*audív*érimus
2	*audiv*isti	*audiv*istis		*audív*eras	*audív*eratis		*audív*eris	*audív*éritis
3	*audiv*it	*audiv*erunt		*audív*erat	*audív*erant		*audív*erit	*audív*erint

♦   The infinitive ending for all 4th conjugation verbs is **ire**.

♦   Verbs followed by (4) are 4th conjugation verbs with regular principal parts.

Vocabulary

Latin	English	Derivative(s)
áudio (4)	to hear	*audition, audio*
dórmio (4)	to sleep	*dormitory*
fínio (4)	to finish, limit	*finish, finite*
múnio (4)	to fortify, protect	*ammunition*
scio (4)	to know	*science*
néscio (4)	to not know	
impédio (4)	to hinder, obstruct	*impede*
vénio venire veni ventus*	to come	*advent*
invénio invenire inveni inventus	to discover, find out	*invent*
séntio sentire sensi sensus	to feel, perceive	*sensitive*

* For the sake of simplicity, the 4th principal part of all verbs is given in **us**.

◆ The regular principal parts for the 4th conjugation are:

1st	2nd	3rd	4th
*aud*io	*aud*ire	*aud*ivi	*aud*itus
I hear	to hear	I heard	heard
io	**ire**	**ivi**	**itus**

◆ Study carefully the three verbs with irregular principal parts. They are written out in full in the vocabulary list.

◆ To find the perfect stem, drop the personal ending **i** from the 3rd principal part, and add the regular endings for the three tenses of the Perfect System.

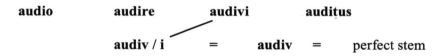

audio	**audire**	**audivi**	**auditus**
	audiv / i	=	**audiv**	=	perfect stem

> Taken from Psalm 71:8, **a mari usque ad mare** is the national motto of Canada. Notice that the saying contains one prepositional object in the accusative (**ad mare**) and one in the ablative (**a mari**).

Oral Drill

1.	**venistis**	1.	they will have come
2.	**invéneras**	2.	we had felt
3.	**sensérimus**	3.	he has discovered
4.	**muniverunt**	4.	you had finished
5.	**scivit**	5.	you all have heard
6.	**finíverint**	6.	she will have hindered
7.	**nescivisti**	7.	we have slept
8.	**vénerat**	8.	I have known
9.	**sénseram**	9.	it has protected
10.	**invénero**	10.	they have not known

Dictum et factum   *Said and done*

3rd Conjugation **io** Verbs   Perfect System

capio capere   to take, capture   *perfect stem* **cep-**

	Perfect			Pluperfect			Future Perfect	
	S.	Pl.		S.	Pl.		S.	Pl.
1	*cep***i**	*cép***imus**		*cép***eram**	*cep***eramus**		*cép***ero**	*cep***érimus**
2	*cep***isti**	*cep***istis**		*cép***eras**	*cep***eratis**		*cép***eris**	*cep***éritis**
3	*cep***it**	*cep***erunt**		*cép***erat**	*cep***erant**		*cép***erit**	*cép***erint**

♦ Verbs are grouped into a conjugation according to the infinitive. All verbs whose infinitive ends in **ere** belong to the 3rd conjugation.

♦ The first principal part of a 3rd **io** verb looks like a 4th conjugation verb, and the present system is identical to 4th conjugation verbs.

♦ There are no regular endings for the principal parts of 3rd **io** verbs. However, notice the similarities in the principal part of **capio, facio,** and **jacio**.

♦ To find the perfect stem, drop the personal ending **i** from the 3rd principal part, and add the regular endings for the three tenses of the Perfect System.

    capio   **capere**   **cepi**   **captus**

          cep / i   **=**   **cep** **=** perfect stem

♦ The Perfect System is perfectly regular in all four conjugations.

Vocabulary

1st	2nd	3rd	4th	Meaning
cápio	**cápere**	**cepi**	**captus**	to take, capture
fácio	**fácere**	**feci**	**factus**	to make, do
jácio	**jácere**	**jeci**	**jactus**	to throw, hurl
fúgio	**fúgere**	**fūgi**	**fugitus***	to flee
cúpio	**cúpere**	**cupivi**	**cupitus**	to desire, wish for

* For the sake of simplicity the 4th principal part of all verbs is given in **us**.

Statue of Cincinnatus with fasces, Cincinnati, Ohio

On the left, Cincinnatus hands back the **fasces** with one hand and grasps the plow with the other, as he relinquishes his power as dictator and resumes his civilian life. The Roman **fasces**, meaning 'bundle,' consisted of a bundle of birch rods with a protruding ax head, all tied with a red leather ribbon. The fasces was the symbol of the Roman Republic's power to punish the evildoer. The fasces, or parts of it, appear in many places in American iconography, including on the Great Seal (grasped by the eagle) and on either side of the podium in the House of Representatives.

Oral Drill

1.	**fecistis**	1.	I had fled
2.	**cupíveram**	2.	she has captured
3.	**jécerint**	3.	they have desired
4.	**fugerunt**	4.	it will have made
5.	**céperit**	5.	you all had hurled
6.	**jécerat**	6.	we have done
7.	**fécimus**	7.	I have fled
8.	**fugérimus**	8.	they will have captured
9.	**cupivit**	9.	you have thrown
10.	**féceras**	10.	they had fled

Quid novi?   *What's new?*

Questions - Interrogative Pronouns and Adverbs

♦ There are two kinds of direct questions in Latin and English.

(1) Questions introduced by question words—interrogative adverbs, adjectives, or pronouns—*who, what, when, where, why, how*. These questions require an answer other than *yes* or *no*. Learn these common question words:

Latin	English
quis?	who?
quid?	what?
quando?	when?
ubi?	where? in what place?
cur?	why?
quot?	how many?
quam diu?	how long?
quomodo?	how (in what manner)?
ne	enclitic to form yes and no questions

and common questions and answers:

Question	English	Answer	English
Quid novi?	What's new?	**Nihil**	Nothing
Quid est tibi nomen?	What is your name?	**Meum praenomen est**	My name is ...
Quomodo vales? [1]	How are you?	**Satis bene.**	Well enough.
		Óptime, grátias.	Very well, thanks.

[1] Conversational Latin also has **Quid Agis** for *How are you?*

(2) Yes or no questions are introduced by the enclitic **ne**, which is added to the end of the first word of the sentence, usually the verb.

Orabat.   He was praying.   **Orabatne?**   Was he praying?

In English we make yes or no questions by placing a helping verb first.

Orabat	He was praying.
Orabatne	Was he praying?
Laborabunt	They will work.
Laborabuntne	Will they work?

There are two tenses which may be translated without helping verbs, the present and perfect. But both of these tenses have two other options with helping verbs. To translate questions in the present or perfect tenses, choose a helping verb and place it first.

Present	**Clamat**	He shouts, he is shouting, he does shout.
	Clamatne	Is he shouting? Does he shout?
Perfect	**Clamavit**	He shouted, he did shout, he has shouted.
	Clamavitne	Did he shout? Has he shouted?

Mosaic
An elaborate depiction of sea life in a mosaic floor of a house in Pompeii.

3rd, 4th, and 3rd **io** Conjugations - Perfect System

Tense	Number	3rd Conj.	4th Conj.	3rd **io** Conj.
Perfect	sing.	*rex*i	*audiv*i	*cep*i
		*rex*isti	*audiv*isti	*cep*isti
		*rex*it	*audiv*it	*cep*it
	pl.	*réx*imus	*audív*imus	*cép*imus
		*rex*istis	*audiv*istis	*cep*istis
		*rex*erunt	*audiv*erunt	*cep*erunt
Pluperfect	sing.	*réx*eram	*audív*eram	*cép*eram
		*réx*eras	*audív*eras	*cép*eras
		*réx*erat	*audiv*erat	*cép*erat
	pl.	*rex*eramus	*audiv*eramus	*cep*eramus
		*rex*eratis	*audiv*eratis	*cep*eratis
		*réx*erant	*audív*erant	*cép*erant
Future Perfect	sing.	*réx*ero	*audív*ero	*cép*ero
		*réx*eris	*audív*eris	*cép*eris
		*réx*erit	*audív*erit	*cép*erit
	pl.	*rex*érimus	*audiv*érimus	*cep*érimus
		*rex*éritis	*audiv*éritis	*cep*éritis
		*réx*erint	*audiv*erint	*cép*erint

Adverbs

Latin	English
quis	who?
quid	what?
quando	when?
ubi	where?
cur	why?
quot	how many?
quam diu	how long?
quomodo	how (in what manner)?

Latin Sayings

Magister dixit.
A mari usque ad mare
Dictum et factum
Quid novi?

Vocabulary

1st	2nd	3rd	4th	Meaning
áudio (4)				to hear
cápio	cápere	cepi	captus	to take, capture
cúpio	cúpere	cupivi	cupitus	to desire
dico	dícere	dixi	dictus	to say, speak, tell
duco	dúcere	duxi	ductus	to lead
dormio (4)				to sleep
fácio	fácere	feci	factus	to make, do
figo	fígere	fixi	fictus	to fix, fasten
finio (4)				to finish
fúgio	fúgere	fugi	fúgitus	to flee
impedio (4)				to hinder, obstruct
invénio	invenire	inveni	inventus	to discover, find out
jácio	jácere	jeci	jactus	to throw, hurl
jungo	júngere	junxi	junctus	to join, connect
munio (4)				to fortify, protect
nescio (4)				to not know
rego	régere	rexi	rectus	to rule
scio (4)				to know
séntio	sentire	sensi	sensus	to feel, perceive
struo	strúere	struxi	structus	to build, construct
traho	tráhere	traxi	tractus	to drag, haul
veho	véhere	vexi	vectus	to convey, carry, transport
vénio	venire	veni	ventus	to come
vinco	víncere	vici	victus	to conquer
vivo	vívere	vixi	victus	to live, be alive

Question	English	Answer	English
Quid novi?	What's new?	Nihil	Nothing
Quid est tibi nomen?	What is your name?	Meum praenomen est	My name is ...
Quomodo vales?[3]	How are you?	Satis bene.	Well enough.
		Óptime, grátias.	Very well, thanks.

♦ The six attributes of a Latin verb are *conjugation, person, number, tense, voice,* and *mood.* In this unit you will learn about **voice**.

♦ Latin and English verbs have two voices, the **active** and the **passive**. All of the verb conjugations you have learned thus far have been in the active voice.

♦ In the active voice, the subject *performs* the action of the verb.

♦ In the passive voice, the subject *receives* the action of the verb.

♦ Here are two sentences that illustrate the active and passive voices:

ACTIVE VOICE

SN   V-t   A   DO
Caesar conquered the Gauls.   The subject, Caesar, performs the action of the verb.

PASSIVE VOICE

A   SN   V-p   P   OP
The Gauls <u>were conquered</u> by Caesar.   The subject, Gauls, receives the action of the verb.

♦ The passive voice of the Present System is formed by substituting the passive personal endings for the active personal endings.

Active personal endings	*Passive personal endings*
o, m	**or, r**
s	**ris**
t	**tur**
mus	**mur**
tis	**mini**
nt	**ntur**

UNIT V

VERBS

PRESENT SYSTEM
PASSIVE INDICATIVE

Supreme Court

The Supreme Court Building in Washington, D.C., is built in the
style of a Greek or Roman temple.

Amicus in necessitate probatur. *A friend is proven in time of necessity.*

1st Conjugation Present Tense Passive Voice

amo amare I love   *present stem* **ama-**

	S	Meaning	Pl.	Meaning
1	*am***or**	*I am loved*	*ama***mur**	*we are loved*
2	*ama***ris**	*you are loved*	*amá***mini**	*you all are loved*
3	*ama***tur**	*he, she, it is loved*	*ama***ntur**	*they are loved*

♦ In the passive voice, the subject does not perform the action of the verb, but rather receives it.

♦ To form the passive voice of the present tense, substitute the passive personal endings for the active personal endings.

Vocabulary

Latin	Gender	English	Derivative(s)
campus -i	*m.*	field, plain	*campus*
cibus -i	*m.*	food	*ciborium*
hortus -i	*m.*	garden	*horticulture*
locus -i	*m.*	place	*location*
ludus -i	*m.*	game, school	*ludicrous*
lupus -i	*m.*	wolf	*lupine*
nimbus -i	*m.*	cloud, storm cloud	*nimbus cloud*
ventus -i	*m.*	wind	*vent*
Gallus -i	*m.*	a Gaul	*Gallic*
Marcus -i	*m.*	Mark	

♦ The active and passive personal endings are:

Active personal endings	Passive personal endings
o, m	**or, r**
s	**ris**
t	**tur**
mus	**mur**
tis	**mini**
nt	**ntur**

♦ Write out the conjugation of **amo** in the present tense. Then go back and rewrite it substituting the passive personal endings for the active personal endings.

♦ The subject is always the focus of the sentence. The sentence below is in the active voice and the focus is on the action of Caesar.

Caesar <u>conquered</u> the Gauls.

The same information written in the passive voice shifts the focus to the Gauls.

The Gauls <u>were conquered</u> by Caesar.

♦ **Ablative of Agent.** In the passive voice the actual person, or LIVING AGENT, who performs the action of the verb may be expressed by a prepositional phrase with the preposition **a/ab** which takes an object in the ablative case.

Galli <u>a Caesare</u> superantur.   The Gauls are conquered <u>by Caesar</u>.

Galli <u>ab hostibus</u> superantur.   The Gauls are conquered <u>by enemies</u>.

The ancient literature is full of aphorisms about friendship. To the Greeks and Romans, true friendship was of the greatest value. Cicero wrote a famous essay **De Amicitia,** *On Friendship.* "A friend," he said, "is another self." You can only be friends with someone you can relate to, someone like yourself.

Nóscitur ex sóciis   *He is known by his companions*

1st Conjugation Passive Voice: Imperfect and Future Tenses

amo amare I love   *present stem* **ama-**

Imperfect tense

	S.	Meaning	Pl.	Meaning
1	*ama*bar	I was being loved	*ama*bamur	we were being loved
2	*ama*baris	you were being loved	*ama*bámini	you all were being loved
3	*ama*batur	h, s, i was being loved	*ama*bantur	they were being loved

Future tense

	S.	Meaning	Pl.	Meaning
1	*ama*bor	I will be loved	*amá*bimur	we will be loved
2	*amá*beris	you will be loved	*ama*bímini	you all will be loved
3	*amá*bitur	h, s, i will be loved	*ama*buntur	they will be loved

Vocabulary

Latin	Gender	English	Derivative(s)
ánimus -i	*m.*	mind, spirit	*animated*
bárbarus -i	*m.*	foreigner, barbarian	*barbarian*
Christianus -i	*m.*	a Christian	*Christian*
discípulus -i	*m.*	student	*disciple*
gládius -i	*m.*	sword	*gladiator*
legatus -i	*m.*	lieutenant	*legate*
óculus -i	*m.*	eye	*binocular*
pópulus -i	*m.*	people	*popular*
Romanus -i	*m.*	a Roman	*Roman*
sócius -i	*m.*	ally	*social*

♦ All that is needed to form the present system passive of all four conjugations is to learn the passive personal endings and practice substituting them for the active personal endings you have always used.

♦ The active and passive personal endings are:

Active personal endings	Passive personal endings
o, m	**or, r**
s	**ris**
t	**tur**
mus	**mur**
tis	**mini**
nt	**ntur**

♦ There is only one irregularity in the whole present passive system. Can you find it? Highlight this form in your book. Say this conjugation aloud repeatedly until you have mastered it.

> **Nóscitur ex sóciis** is a proverbial expression in many cultures.
> In English we might say, "You are judged by the company you keep."

Oral Drill

1.	**vocatur**	1.	I am carried
2.	**culpantur**	2.	we are loved
3.	**portabar**	3.	they are attacked
4.	**amaris**	4.	you are judged
5.	**occupamur**	5.	you all are helped
6.	**dubitámini**	6.	it will be given
7.	**dabuntur**	7.	they will be explored
8.	**juváberis**	8.	she is washed
9.	**judicabamur**	9.	we were being praised
10.	**accusabantur**	10.	I will be blamed

Ferrum ferro exacúitur   *Iron is sharpened by iron*
Proverbs 27:17

2nd Conjugation   Present System   Passive Voice

moneo monére   I warn   *present stem*   **mone-**

	Present		Imperfect		Future	
	S.	Pl.	S.	Pl.	S.	Pl.
1	*móne**or***	*mone**mur***	*mone**bar***	*mone**bamur***	*mone**bor***	*moné**bimur***
2	*mone**ris***	*moné**mini***	*mone**baris***	*mone**bámini***	*moné**beris***	*mone**bímini***
3	*mone**tur***	*mone**ntur***	*mone**batur***	*mone**bantur***	*moné**bitur***	*mone**buntur***

◆ The passive voice of the 2nd conjugation is formed according to the same principles as the 1st conjugation. Write out the conjugation of **móneo** in the present system. Then go back and rewrite it, substituting the passive personal endings for the active personal endings. Say this conjugation aloud repeatedly until you have mastered it.

Vocabulary

Latin	Gender	English	Derivative(s)
argentum -i	*n.*	silver	*Argentina*
aurum -i	*n.*	gold	
collum -i	*n.*	neck	*collar*
ferrum -i	*n.*	iron, tool made of iron	
lignum -i	*n.*	wood	*lignite*
scutum -i	*n.*	shield	*escutcheon*
telum -i	*n.*	missile (javelin, spear, dart)	
tergum -i	*n.*	back, rear	
vallum -i	*n.*	wall, rampart	
vinum -i	*n.*	wine	

◆ Note the same irregularity in the 2nd person singular of the future tense, where the ending is **beris** rather than **biris**. Highlight this form in your book.

◆ **Ablative of Means.** The ablative <u>without a preposition</u> is used to express the NON-LIVING agent, the means, or the instrument of the action. The noun in the ablative case can be translated with the prepositions *by* or *with*, with the precise meaning, *by means of.*

<u>Voice</u>

passive	**Púeri <u>gládio</u> terrentur.**	The boys are frightened <u>by the sword</u>.
passive	**Pópulus <u>verbis</u> movetur**	The people are moved <u>by the words</u>.
active	**Romani óppidum <u>gládiis</u> vincunt.**	The Romans conquer the town <u>with swords</u>.

> **Ferrum ferro exacúitur** is a good example of the passive voice and the ablative of means. The complete verse from the Latin Bible, The Vulgate, is a commentary on friendship with the meaning, "As iron is sharpened by iron, so man is sharpened by his friends."

Oral Drill

1.	videtur	1.	I am held
2.	prohibentur	2.	we are ordered
3.	terreor	3.	they are warned
4.	teneris	4.	you are seen
5.	monemur	5.	you all are held
6.	docémini	6.	it will be frightened
7.	jubebuntur	7.	they will be moved
8.	terreberis	8.	she is moved
9.	videbamur	9.	we were being taught
10.	movebantur	10.	I will be ordered

Repetítio mater studiorum   *Repetition is the mother of learning*

jaceo
habeo
taceo

3rd Conjugation   Present System   Passive Voice

rego régere I rule   *present stem* **reg-**

Present		Imperfect		Future	
S.	Pl.	S.	Pl.	S.	Pl.
1	*reg*or	*rég*imur	*reg*ebar	*reg*ebamur	*reg*ar	*reg*emur
2	*rég*eris	*reg*ímini	*reg*ebaris	*reg*ebámini	*reg*eris	*reg*émini
3	*rég*itur	*reg*untur	*reg*ebatur	*reg*ebantur	*reg*etur	*reg*entur

♦ The passive of the 3rd conjugation is formed according to the same principles as the 1st and 2nd conjugations. Write out the conjugation of **rego** in the present system. Then go back and rewrite it substituting the passive personal endings for the active personal endings. Say this conjugation aloud repeatedly until you have mastered it.

Vocabulary

Latin	Gender	English	Derivative(s)
brácchium -i	*n.*	arm (forearm)	*brachium (anatomy)*
fólium -i	*n.*	leaf	*folio, foliage*
frumentum -i	*n.*	grain, corn	
gáudium -i	*n.*	joy	*gaudy*
peccatum -i	*n.*	sin, mistake	*peccadillo*
praémium -i	*n.*	reward	*premium*
proélium -i	*n.*	battle	
saéculum -i	*n.*	age, time period	*secular*
signum -i	*n.*	sign	*signal*
stúdium -i	*n.*	zeal, enthusiasm, study	*studious*

♦ Notice the irregularity in the 2nd person singular of the present tense, **régeris** rather than the expected **regiris**. Highlight this form in your book.

♦ Although the 3rd conjugation passive voice is formed exactly the same as the 1st and 2nd conjugations, the similarities between the 3rd conjugation present and future tenses make mastery of this system much more difficult. Diligence and persistence must be applied in learning these forms.

♦ Note also that the 2nd person singular of both the present and future tenses are identical except for the accent mark on the present tense form. These two forms are distinguished audibly and visually by the accented syllable.

<u>2nd P. Sing.</u>

present tense	**régeris**	RE ge ris
future tense	**regeris**	re GE ris

> From St. Thomas Aquinas, **Repetítio mater studiorum** was the motto of the Jesuits who began each lesson with a recitation of the previous lesson and ended each lesson with a recitation of the work just completed. The primary meaning of the word **stúdium** is *enthusiasm* or *zeal*. Repetition is the source of enthusiasm for learning.

Oral Drill

1.	**trahor**	1.	we will be hauled
2.	**dicuntur**	2.	I am told
3.	**regímini**	3.	she is ruled
4.	**júngimur**	4.	it was being built
5.	**strúitur**	5.	you all are joined
6.	**vínceris**	6.	you were being led
7.	**vinceris**	7.	I am fastened
8.	**figebantur**	8.	they are conveyed
9.	**vehetur**	9.	we were being conquered
10.	**ducuntur**	10.	I will be conquered

Cápitur urbs quae totum cepit orbem.
The city which captured the whole world is now captured.

4th Conjugation   Present System   Passive Voice

audio audire I hear   *present stem* **audi**

	Present			Imperfect			Future	
	S.	Pl.		S.	Pl.		S.	Pl.
1	*áudi* or	*audi* mur		*audi* ebar	*audi* ebamur		*áudi* ar	*audi* emur
2	*audi* ris	*audí* mini		*audi* ebaris	*audi* ebámini		*audi* eris	*audi* émini
3	*audi* tur	*audi* untur		*audi* ebatur	*audi* ebantur		*audi* etur	*audi* entur

♦ 3rd declension nouns ending in **or-oris** are usually masculine. But since trees are generally feminine, **arbor árboris** is an exception to this gender rule.

♦ The passive of 3rd **io** and 4th conjugation verbs is formed according to the same principles as the 1st conjugation.

Vocabulary

Latin	Gender	English	Derivative(s)
arbor árboris	*f.*	tree	*arbor, arboretum*
amor amoris	*m.*	love, passion	*amorous*
clamor -oris	*m.*	shout, cry	*clamorous*
dolor -oris	*m.*	grief, pain	*dolorous*
imperator -oris	*m.*	general, commander	*imperious*
labor -oris	*m.*	work, toil	*laborious*
orator -oris	*m.*	speaker, orator	*oratory*
pastor -oris	*m.*	shepherd, pastor	*pastoral*
piscator -oris	*m.*	fisherman	*pisces*
senator -oris	*m.*	senator	

3rd io Conjugation   Present System   Passive Voice

capio cápere *I take*   *present stem* **capi**

Present			Imperfect			Future	
S.	Pl.		S.	Pl.		S.	Pl.
1	*cápi*or	*cápi*mur	*capi*ebar	*capi*ebamur	*cápi*ar	*capi*emur
2	*cáp*eris	*capí*mini	*capi*ebaris	*capi*ebámini	*capi*eris	*capi*émini
3	*cápi*tur	*capi*untur	*capi*ebatur	*capi*ebantur	*capi*etur	*capi*entur

◆ NOTICE the 2nd person singular of the present tense for both conjugations. The 3rd **io** verbs follow the irregular pattern of the 3rd conjugation, but the 4th conjugation does not.

Cápitur urbs quae totum cepit orbem. According to tradition, in A.D. 410, when Rome fell to Alaric the Goth, St. Jerome pushed aside his translation of the Book of Ezekiel and cried out in anguish as he wrote these poignant words. Even Christians thought the Roman Empire would last forever—after they had converted it to a Christian state.

But St. Augustine had a different response to the capture of Rome by the Goths. It is said this event was the motivation for his great work, *City of God*, in which he develops his Christian philosophy of history: All human cities are born in blood and violence and all are destined to die, even Rome. There is only one eternal city, the City of God, established by Christ, and destined to endure until he comes again.

St. Jerome

A medieval depiction of St. Jerome in his study by Italian Renaissance painter Domenico Ghirlandaio.

77

Present System Passive Voice

Tense		1st Conj.	2nd Conj.	3rd Conj.	4th Conj.	3rd **io** Conj.
Present	sing.	*am* **or** *ama* **ris** *ama* **tur**	*móne* **or** *mone* **ris** *mone* **tur**	*reg* **or** *rég* **eris** *rég* **itur**	*áudi* **or** *audi* **ris** *audi* **tur**	*cápi* **or** *cáp* **eris** *cápi* **tur**
	pl.	*ama* **mur** *amá* **mini** *ama* **ntur**	*mone* **mur** *moné* **mini** *mone* **ntur**	*rég* **imur** *reg* **ímini** *reg* **untur**	*audí* **mur** *audí* **mini** *audi* **untur**	*cápi* **mur** *capí* **mini** *capi* **untur**
Imperfect	sing.	*ama* **bar** *ama* **baris** *ama* **batur**	*mone* **bar** *mone* **baris** *mone* **batur**	*reg* **ebar** *reg* **ebaris** *reg* **ebatur**	*audi* **ebar** *audi* **ebaris** *audi* **ebatur**	*capi* **ebar** *capi* **ebaris** *capi* **ebatur**
	pl.	*ama* **bamur** *ama* **bámini** *ama* **bantur**	*mone* **bamur** *mone* **bámini** *mone* **bantur**	*reg* **ebamur** *reg* **ebámini** *reg* **ebantur**	*audi* **ebamur** *audi* **ebámini** *audi* **ebantur**	*capi* **ebamur** *capi* **ebámini** *capi* **ebantur**
Future	sing.	*ama* **bor** *amá* **beris** *amá* **bitur**	*mone* **bor** *moné* **beris** *moné* **bitur**	*reg* **ar** *reg* **eris** *reg* **etur**	*áudi* **ar** *audi* **eris** *audi* **etur**	*cápi* **ar** *capi* **eris** *capi* **etur**
	pl.	*amá* **bimur** *ama* **bímini** *ama* **buntur**	*moné* **bimur** *mone* **bímini** *mone* **buntur**	*reg* **emur** *reg* **émini** *reg* **entur**	*audi* **emur** *audi* **émini** *audi* **entur**	*capi* **emur** *capi* **émini** *capi* **entur**

All irregularities occur in the **2nd Person Singular**,

Conj.	Tense	P & N	Irregularity		
1st	future	2nd sing.	**amáberis**	*not*	amabiris
2nd	future	2nd sing.	**monéberis**	*not*	monebiris

3rd	present	2nd sing.	**régeris**	*not*	regiris
3rd **io**	present	2nd sing.	**cáperis**	*not*	capiris

Conj.	Tense	P & N	NOT Irregular!!!
4th	present	2nd sing.	**audiris**

Vocabulary Review

amor amoris *m.*	love, passion	**Gallus -i** *m.*	a Gaul	**piscator -oris** *m.*	fisherman
ánimus -i *m.*	mind, spirit	**gáudium -i** *n.*	joy	**pópulus -i** *m.*	people
arbor árboris *f.*	tree	**gládius -i** *m.*	sword	**praémium -i** *n.*	reward
argentum -i *n.*	silver	**hortus -i** *m.*	garden	**proélium -i** *n.*	battle
aurum -i *n.*	gold	**imperator -oris** *m.*	general, commander	**Romanus -i** *m.*	a Roman
bárbarus -i *m.*	barbarian, foreigner	**labor -oris** *m.*	work, toil	**saéculum -i** *n.*	age, time period
brácchium -i *n.*	forearm	**legatus -i** *m.*	lieutenant	**scutum -i** *n.*	shield
campus -i *m.*	field, plain	**lignum -i.** *n.*	wood	**senator -oris** *m.*	senator
Christianus -i *m.*	a Christian	**locus -i** *m.*	place, location	**signum -i** *n.*	sign
cibus -i *m.*	food	**ludus -i** *m.*	school, game	**sócius -i** *m.*	ally
clamor -oris *m.*	shout, cry	**lupus -i** *m.*	wolf	**stúdium -i** *n.*	zeal, study, enthusiasm
collum -i *n.*	neck	**Marcus -i** *m.*	Mark	**telum -i** *n.*	missile
discípulus -i *m.*	student	**nimbus -i** *m.*	cloud, storm cloud	**tergum -i** *n.*	back, rear
dolor -oris *m.*	grief, pain	**óculus -i** *m.*	eye	**vallum -i** *n.*	wall, rampart
ferrum -i *n.*	iron, tool	**orator -oris** *m.*	orator	**ventus -i** *m.*	wind
fólium -i *n.*	leaf	**pastor -oris** *m.*	shepherd, pastor	**vinum -i** *n.*	wine
frumentum -i *n.*	grain, corn	**peccatum -i** *n.*	sin, mistake		

Syntax Review

Ablative of Agent. A/ab with the ablative is used to express the LIVING AGENT that performs the action of the verb.

Ablative of Means. The ablative <u>without</u> a preposition is used to express the NON-LIVING agent, means, or instrument of the action of the verb.

Third Declension Gender Rules: Nouns ending in **x** are usually feminine. Nouns ending in **or-oris** are usually masculine.

Latin Sayings

Amicus in necessitate probatur.   Nóscitur ex sóciis
Ferrum ferro exacúitur   Repetítio mater studiorum
Cápitur urbs quae totum cepit orbem.

APPENDICES

Everyday Latin

Salve (salvete)*	*Greetings, hello*
Vale (valete)	*Good bye*
Quid est nomen tibi?	*What is your name?*
Mihi nomen est ...	*My name is ...*
Quid agis?	*How are you?*
Valeo.	*I am well.*
Admirábilis	*Wonderful*
Grátias tibi ago.	*Thank you.*
Optatus venis.	*You are most welcome.*
Ignosce mihi, quaeso.	*Pardon (excuse) me, please.*
Sodes	*Please (would you mind, if you don't mind)*
Me paénitet.	*I'm sorry.*
Te amo.	*I love you.*
(Ego amo te.)	*I love you. (Not as correct but a student favorite)*
Ita.	*Yes.*

Classroom Latin

Salvete, amici Latinae.	*Greetings, friends of Latin.*
Salvete, discípuli.	*Hello, students.*
Salve, magister/magistra. *(m/f)*	*Greetings (hello), teacher.*
Salve, discípule.	*Hello, student.*
Vale, magister/magistra. *(m/f)*	*Good bye, teacher.*
Valete, discípuli.	*Good bye, students.*
Sede (sedete).	*Sit down.*
Surge (súrgite).	*Stand up.*
Adsum	*Present*
Aperi (aperite)	*Open*
Claude (claúdite)	*Close*
jánuam	*door*
fenestram, fenestras	*window, windows*
librum, libros	*book, books*

*The words in parenthesis are plural commands or greetings.

Audi (audite) diligenter	*Listen carefully*
Impossíbile est.	*That is impossible.*
Est-ne confusus?	*Are you puzzled?*
Explica, quaeso.	*Please explain.*
Non intéllego.	*I don't understand.*
Adjuva (adjuvate) me.	*Help me.*
Fallit.	*It is wrong.*
Falsus	*Wrong, incorrect*
Verum	*Correct*
Siléntium, quaeso	*Silence, please*
Tace (tacete)	*Be silent*
Ad páginam	*Turn to page*
Responde mihi	*Answer me*
Oremus.	*Let us pray.*
Bene actum.	*Well done.*
Óptime!	*Excellent!*
Péssime!	*Very bad!*
Scribe (scribite) haec verba	*Write these words*
Fiat.	*All right (let it be done).*
De hoc satis!	*Enough of this!*
Collige fólia.	*Collect the papers.*
Quid dixit? dixisti?	*What did he say? you say?*

Signum Crucis

In nómine Patris et Fílii et Spíritus Sancti.

Pater Noster

Pater Noster, Qui es in Caelis. Sanctificetur Nomen Tuum. Advéniat Regnum Tuum, fiat voluntas Tua, sicut in Caelo et in terra. Panem nostrum cotidianum da nobis hódie. Et dímitte nobis débita nostra, sicut et nos dimíttimus debitóribus nostris et ne nos inducas in tentationem, sed líbera nos a malo.

Table Blessing

Benedíc Dómine nos et haec tua dona quae de tua largitate sumus sumpturi.

Per Christum Dóminum Nostrum. Amen.

Doxology (Gloria Patri)

Glória Patri et Fílio et Spíritui Sancto. Sicut erat in princípio et nunc et semper et in saécula saeculorum. Amen

Sanctus and Benedictus

Sanctus, Sanctus, Sanctus, Dóminus Deus Sábaoth. Pleni sunt Caeli et terra glória Tua.

Hosanna in Excelsis. Benedictus qui venit in nómine Dómini. Hosanna in Excelsis.

Agnus Dei

Agnus Dei, qui tollis peccata mundi, miserere nobis.
Agnus Dei, qui tollis peccata mundi, miserere nobis.
Agnus Dei, qui tollis peccata mundi, dona nobis pacem.

Ave Maria

Ave Maria, grátia plena, Dóminus tecum. Benedicta tu in muliéribus, et benedictus fructus ventris tui, Jesus.

Sancta Maria, Mater Dei, ora pro nobis peccatóribus. Nunc et in hora mortis nostrae. Amen.

Sign of the Cross

In the name of the Father, the Son and the Holy Ghost.

Our Father

Our Father who art in Heaven. Hallowed be thy name. Thy kingdom come, thy will be done, on earth as it is in heaven. Give us this day our daily bread and forgive us our trespasses as we forgive those who trespass against us, and lead us not into temptation but deliver us from evil.

Table Blessing

Bless us O Lord and these thy gifts which we are about to receive from thy bounty. Through Christ Our Lord, Amen.

Doxology

Glory be to the Father, and to the Son, and to the Holy Spirit. As it was in the beginning, is now and ever shall be, world without end. Amen.

Sanctus and Benedictus

Holy, Holy, Holy, Lord God of Hosts. Heaven and earth are full of Your glory Hosanna in the highest. Blessed is he who comes in the name of the Lord Hosanna in the highest.

Agnus Dei

Lamb of God, you take away the sins of the world, have mercy on us.
Lamb of God, you take away the sins of the world, have mercy on us.
Lamb of God, you take away the sins of the world, grant us peace.

Hail Mary

Hail Mary, full of grace, The Lord is with thee, Blessed art thou among women And blessed is the fruit of thy womb, Jesus.

Holy Mary, Mother of God, Pray for us sinners, Now and at the hour of our death. Amen.

alma mater*	nurturing mother
Anno Dómini (A.D.)*	In the year of our Lord
ante bellum *	before the war
Caput Mundi	Head of the World
Carpe diem.	Seize the day.
Cave canem.	Beware the dog.
Civis Romanus sum.	I am a Roman citizen.
Docēre, delectare, movēre	To teach, to delight, to move
Errare est humanum.	To err is human.
Fortes fortuna juvat.	Fortune aids the brave.
In choro recitémus.	Let us recite together.
In umbra, ígitur, pugnábimus.	Then we will fight in the shade.
Mater Itáliae Roma*	The mother of Italy, Rome
nunc aut numquam*	now or never
Ora et labora.*	Pray and work.
Pax Romana*	The Roman Peace
Quattuor anni témpora	The four seasons of the year
Rex Regum	King of Kings
Roma Aeterna	Eternal Rome
semper fidelis*	always faithful
Senatus Populusque Romanus (S.P.Q.R.)*	The Senate and People of Rome
Stabat Mater	The Mother was Standing
Veni, vidi, vici.*	I came, I saw, I conquered.
Vídeo et táceo.	I see and am silent.

*Sayings also in *Latina Christiana I*

A mari usque ad mare	*From sea to sea*
Ab Urbe Cóndită	*from the founding of the city*
Ad astra per áspera.	*To the stars through difficulties.*
Ager Vaticanus	*The Vatican Field*
Amicus in necessitate probatur.	*A friend is proven in time of necessity.*
Ars longa vita brevis.	*Art is long and life is short.*
Aut viam invéniam aut fáciam.	*I shall either find a way or make one.*
Cápitur urbs quae totum cepit orbem.	*The city which captured the whole world is now captured.*
Dictum et factum	*Said and done*
Ego sum via et véritas et vita.	*I am the way, the truth, and the life.*
Et tu, Brute?*	*You too, Brutus?*
Ferrum ferro exacúitur	*Iron is sharpened by iron*
Festina lentē	*Make haste slowly*
Hánnibal ad portas	*Hannibal at the gates*
In hoc signo vinces.	*In this sign you will conquer.*
Magister dixit.	*The master has spoken.*
Mare Nostrum	*Our Sea*
mea culpa*	*my fault*
Nóscitur ex sóciis	*He is known by his companions*
Quid novi?	*What's new?*
Repetítio mater studiorum	*Repetition is the mother of learning*
Tempus fugit	*Time flies*

*Sayings also in *Latina Christiana I*

A sentence is a complete thought and is made of two basic parts, the **subject** and the **predicate**.

Mary   **walks.**

subject   predicate

The subject is **what** or **who** the sentence is about.
The predicate tells what the subject **is** or **does**.

The *complete subject* contains the subject with all of its modifiers. The *simple subject* is usually just called the subject. The *complete predicate* contains the simple predicate and its modifiers. The simple predicate is called the *verb*. Modifiers in the subject and predicate do not change the basic structure of the sentence.

simple subject   simple predicate (main verb with helping verbs)

Shouting with joy, Mary   **was skipping through the garden yesterday.**
complete subject   complete predicate

One way to help students understand grammar is to label each word in a sentence. Here is a list of sentence parts and their abbreviations. Students can write these abbreviations above each word and then diagram each sentence. Here are the labels that will be used in this text.

Subject noun	SN
Subject pronoun	SP
Subject (personal ending - Latin verb)	SPE
Verb	V
Verb-transitive	V-t
Linking verb	LV
Article	A
Adjective	Adj
Adverb	Adv
Predicate adjective	PA
Predicate nominative	PrN
Direct object	DO
Complementary infinitive	CI
Indirect Object	IO
Preposition	P
Object of a Preposition	OP

Action Verbs

Action verbs express action, either seen, such as *do, run, write,* and *go,* or unseen, such as *think, believe,* and *know.*

Action verbs can be *transitive* or *intransitive.* Most verbs are transitive because they express action that can be passed from the subject to another person or thing in the sentence, the direct object.

SN   V-t   DO
Ben eats the sandwich.

Eat is a transitive verb because the action is passed from the subject to the direct object, the *sandwich.*

Some verbs, by their nature, cannot take a direct object.

Ben is sleeping. Ben will arrive late.

Sleep and *arrive* are intransitive. The action cannot be passed on to another person or thing in the sentence. (*Late* is an adverb, not a direct object.)

Some verbs are exclusively transitive or intransitive, but most can be either.

State of Being Verbs

A state of being verb expresses existence or state of being. It does not express action, and therefore by definition is *intransitive.*

The most common state of being verb is the *to be* verb, whose forms in English are *am, is, are, was, were, be, being, been.*

The *to be* verb is usually a linking verb, linking the subject to a word in the predicate that names or describes the subject.

SN LV   PrN   SN LV PA
Ben was a soldier.   Ben is strong.

In these sentences the noun that renames the subject is called the predicate nominative (PrN), and the adjective that describes the subject is called the predicate adjective (PA).

There are seven basic sentence patterns. Four were presented in *First Form,* all of which are repeated here. The fifth sentence pattern is included in this text.

Diagramming

Diagramming gives students a picture of sentence structure, and is another effective technique to help students understand grammar The diagram begins with a horizontal line that contains the backbone of the sentence—the subject and the verb. Crossing over this line is a vertical line that divides the sentence into its two parts, the simple subject on the left and the verb on the right. Adjectives and adverbs are written on slanted lines below the words they modify.

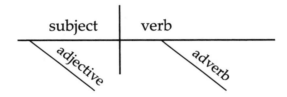

Complements are written on the horizontal line and separated from the verb by a line which <u>does not</u> cross over the base line. If the complement is a direct object, the vertical line is perpendicular to the base line.

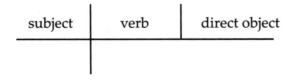

If the complement is a predicate nominative or adjective, the vertical line is slanted to the left.

Sentence Pattern #1
Subject + Verb

If an action verb is intransitive, all that is needed for a sentence is the backbone—a subject and a verb. The subject can be a noun or a pronoun, and other modifiers such as adverbs and adjectives do not change the basic pattern.

The verb can be one word or it can be a verb phrase. A verb phrase contains a main verb plus all of its helping verbs. In this text we will underline the verb phrase when labeling sentences.

SN   V   Adv.
Mary <u>is walking</u> today.

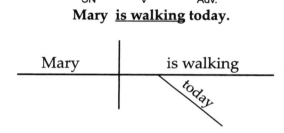

In Latin, the subject of a sentence can be the personal ending of the verb (SPE). Here is a model for diagramming and labeling this kind of sentence in both English and Latin.

V   SPE   SP   V
Ambul(o)   **I walk.**

(o) | ambulo   I | walk

Sentence Patterns #2 through #5

Sentence Pattern #1 above is the only one of the seven basic sentence patterns that does <u>not</u> have **complements**. Most verbs need a completer to *complete* their meaning. If I say *Mary likes*, you do not feel like I have finished my thought. You want to know *what Mary likes*. All of the six remaining sentence patterns have complements. Four are included in this text: the *direct object, predicate nominative, predicate adjective,* and *indirect object.*

Sentence Pattern #2
Subject + Verb + Direct Object

The first type of complement is the direct object. Typical English word order is *subject-verb-direct object*. Typical Latin word order is *subject-direct object-verb*. Diagramming follows English word order.

The direct object can be a noun or pronoun ...

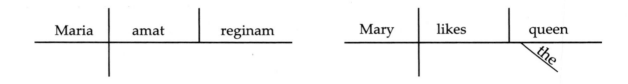

| SN   DO   V-t | SN   V-t   DO |
| **Maria reginam amat.** | **Mary likes the queen.** |

or other more complex constructions, such as the *Complementary Infinitive (CI)*.

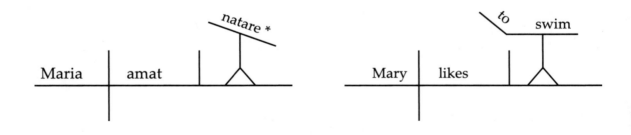

| SN   CI   V-t | SN   V-t   CI |
| **Maria natare amat.** | **Mary likes <u>to swim</u>.** |

* We are using a single slanted line here because "to swim" is one word in Latin.

Sentence Pattern #3
Subject + Verb + Predicate Adjective

Verbs that are completed by a predicate nominative or adjective are called *linking verbs*. They are *intransitive* because they are not completed by a direct object. If an adjective follows the linking verb and describes the subject, it is called a *predicate adjective* and is in the nominative case.

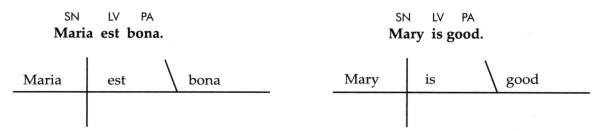

Sentence Pattern #4
Subject + Verb + Predicate Nominative

If a noun follows the linking verb and renames the subject, it is called a *predicate nominative* and is in the nominative case.

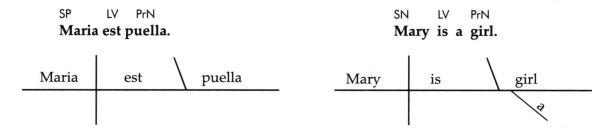

Again modifiers do not change the basic sentence pattern.

SN LV   Adj. PrN Adv.
Mary is a good girl today.

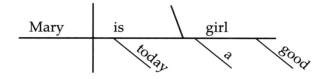

Sentence Pattern #5
Subject + Verb + Indirect Object + Direct Object

Sentences that have direct objects may also have an indirect object. Verbs that typically have indirect objects are giving and telling verbs. In Latin the indirect object usually precedes the direct object and is in the dative case, as shown below. To diagram an indirect object, draw a slanted line under the verb and write the indirect object on a connecting horizontal line.

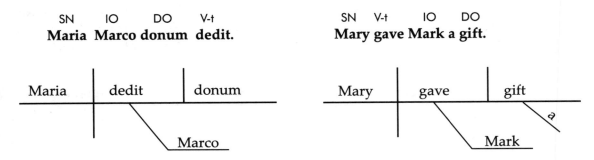

English often uses a prepositional phrase for the indirect object, but this is not done in Latin. Regardless of how the indirect object is written in English, in Latin it is put into the dative case. The sentence below means exactly the same thing as the English sentence above and is translated into Latin the same way.

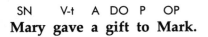

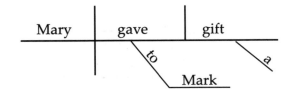

◆ English and Latin don't have a one-to-one correspondence between their verb tenses. Beginning students should memorize a meaning for each Latin tense. Later they will study them more thoroughly to learn how to translate correctly between the two languages. English often has a verb phrase of 2-4 words that requires only one word in Latin.

◆ English has progressive forms in every tense to show continuous action. Latin does not.

◆ The main difficulty lies in the English past and the Latin perfect and imperfect. Study carefully the second and fourth rows, the English past and present perfect. Notice that the simple past in English, *I called every hour*, requires the imperfect tense in Latin.

English Tenses	Examples	Use in Latin and English	Corresponding Latin Tenses and examples
Present System			
Present 　Simple 　Progressive 　Emphatic	I *call* home. I *am calling* now. I *do call*.	General statement Ongoing present action Emphasis	Present 　　**Voco**
Past 　Simple 　Progressive 　Emphatic	I *called* home. I *called* every hour. I *was calling*. I *did call*.	Indefinite past time Repeated past action Ongoing past action Emphasis	Perfect　**Vocavi** Imperfect **Vocabam** Imperfect **Vocabam** Perfect　**Vocavi**
Future 　Progressive	I *will call*. I *will be calling*.	Future action	Future　**Vocabo**
Perfect System			
Present Perfect 　Progressive	I *have called*. I *have been calling* all day.	Completed action with respect to a present action, or a past action continuing to the present	Perfect　**Vocavi**
Past Perfect 　Progressive	I *had called* when you arrived. I *had been calling*.	Completed action with respect to a past action	Pluperfect 　　**Vocaveram**
Future Perfect 　Progressive	I *will have called*. I *will have been calling*.	A future action completed with respect to another future action	Future Perfect 　　**Vocavero**

A pronoun is a word that takes the place of a noun. The word to which the pronoun refers, or takes the place of, is called the antecedent. Learn pronoun names in these pairs to make them easy to remember.

1. **Personal and Possessive Pronouns**
   The possessive pronouns are just the possessive forms of personal pronouns.

   Personal: Subject forms: *I, we, you, he, she, it, they*
   Object forms: *me, us, you, him, her, it, them*

   Possessive: Adjective forms: *my, our, your, her, his, its, their*
   Noun forms: *mine, ours, yours, hers, his, its, theirs*

   Examples:

   My hat is on the table.   *My* is used as a possessive pronoun adjective.
   Mine is on the rack.   *Mine* is used as a possessive pronoun.

2. **Reflexive and Intensive Pronouns**
   Personal pronouns combined with self or selves can be used as reflexive or intensive pronouns, which in English have the same forms, but different in Latin.

   Forms: *myself, ourselves, yourself, yourselves, himself, herself, itself, themselves*

   Reflexive pronouns reflect back on the subject: He hit *himself* on the foot.

   Intensive pronouns add emphasis: Caesar *himself* led the charge.

3. **Interrogative and Relative Pronouns**

   Interrogative pronouns: *who, whom, which, what, whose*

   An **interrogative** pronoun is used in questions. *Whose* and *which* can be used as interrogative adjectives also. Examples:

   > Whose is that?
   > Whose scarf is that?
   > Who are you?
   > Whom do you want?

   Relative pronouns: *who, whom, which, that, whose*

   A **relative** pronoun introduces a relative adjective clause. The relative pronoun refers back to its antecedent, connects its clause to the main clause, and performs a function in its own clause.

   > Caesar is the general *who* conquered Gaul.
   > Gaul is the country *that* Caesar conquered.
   > Caesar is a general *whom* we can trust.
   > Caesar is a general *whose* ambition is well known.
   > The ambition for *which* Caesar was famous led to his death.

4. **Demonstrative and Indefinite Pronouns**

These two kinds of pronouns are not related like the other three pairs. They are just the two that are left over.

Demonstrative pronouns point out things or persons. They can be used as pronouns or adjectives. Forms: *this, that, these, those*

I like *this* book.   This is an adjective.
I like *this*.   This is a pronoun.

Indefinite pronouns usually express the idea of quantity. See below for common ones.

Pronoun Type	English Forms	Latin Forms
Personal	I, me, we, us you, you all he, him, she, her it, they, them	ego, mei tu, tui is, ea, id
Possessive	my, mine our, ours your, yours your, yours his own, her own, their own his, her, hers, its, their, theirs	meus, mea, meum noster, tra, trum tuus, tua, tuum vester, tra, trum suus, a, um *or* ejus, eorum, earum
Reflexive	myself, ourselves yourself, yourselves himself, herself, itself, themselves	sui, sibi, se, se
Intensive	same as above	ipse, ipsa, ipsum
Interrogative pronoun **Interrogative adjective**	who, whom, which, what, whose which, what, whose	quis, quis, quid qui, quae, quod
Relative pronoun **Relative adjective**	who, whom, which, that, whose which, that, whose	qui, quae, quod qui, quae, quod
Demonstrative	this, these that, those	hic, haec, hoc ille, illa, illud *or* is, ea, id
Indefinite	all, each, most, other another, either, neither, several any, everybody, nobody, some anybody, everyone, none, somebody anyone, few, no one, someone both, many, one, such	omnis, quisque, quidque aliquis aliquid alius alia aliud ullus -a -um quisquam quidquam *etc.*

NOUNS – THE FIVE DECLENSIONS

First Declension

Feminine	
S.	Pl.
mensa	mensae
mensae	mensarum
mensae	mensis
mensam	mensas
mensa	mensis

Second Declension

Masculine		Neuter	
S.	Pl.	S.	Pl.
servus	servi	bellum	bella
servi	servorum	belli	bellorum
servo	servis	bello	bellis
servum	servos	bellum	bella
servo	servis	bello	bellis

Third Declension

Masculine/Feminine		Neuter	
S.	Pl.	S.	Pl.
pater	patres	flumen	flúmina
patris	patrum	flúminis	flúminum
patri	pátribus	flúmini	flumínibus
patrem	patres	flumen	flúmina
patre	pátribus	flúmine	fluminibus

Fourth Declension

Masculine	
S.	Pl.
portus	portus
portus	pórtuum
pórtui	pórtibus
portum	portus
portu	pórtibus

Fifth Declension

Feminine	
S.	Pl.
res	res
rei	rerum
rei	rebus
rem	res
re	rebus

ADDITIONAL NOUNS OF THE SECOND AND THIRD DECLENSIONS

ER - IR Nouns of the Second Declension

Masculine		Masculine		Masculine	
S.	Pl.	S.	Pl.	S.	Pl.
ager	agri	puer	púeri	vir	viri
agri	agrorum	púeri	puerorum	viri	virorum
agro	agris	púero	púeris	viro	viris
agrum	agros	púerum	púeros	virum	viros
agro	agris	púero	púeris	viro	viris

Third Declension i-stems

Masculine/Feminine		Neuter	
S.	Pl.	S.	Pl.
pars	partes	mare	mária
partis	pártium	maris	márium
parti	pártibus	mari	máribus
partem	partes	mare	mária
parte	pártibus	mari	máribus

Personal Pronouns

Case	First Person		Second Person	
	S.	Pl.	S.	Pl.
nom.	ego	nos	tu	vos
gen.	mei	nostri, nostrum	tui	vestri, vestrum
dat.	mihi	nobis	tibi	vobis
acc.	me	nos	te	vos
abl.	me	nobis	te	vobis

ADJECTIVES

First and Second Declension Adjectives

Case	Singular			Plural		
	M.	F.	N.	M.	F.	N.
nom.	bonus	bona	bonum	boni	bonae	bona
gen.	boni	bonae	boni	bonorum	bonarum	bonorum
dat.	bono	bonae	bono	bonis	bonis	bonis
acc.	bonum	bonam	bonum	bonos	bonas	bona
abl.	bono	bonā	bono	bonis	bonis	bonis

First and Second Declension **er** Adjectives

Case	Singular			Plural		
	M.	F.	N.	M.	F.	N.
nom.	liber	líbera	líberum	líberi	líberae	líbera
gen.	líberi	líberae	líberi	liberorum	liberarum	liberorum
dat.	líbero	liberae	líbero	líberis	líberis	líberis
acc.	líberum	líberam	líberum	líberos	líberas	líbera
abl.	líbero	líberā	líbero	líberis	líberis	líberis

Third Declension Adjectives

Case	Singular		Plural	
	M./F.	N.	M./F.	N.
nom.	brevis	breve	breves	brévia
gen.	brevis	brevis	brévium	brévium
dat.	brevi	brevi	brévibus	brévibus
acc.	brevem	breve	breves	brévia
abl.	brevi	brevi	brévibus	brévibus

Active Indicative of the Four Conjugations and Sum

Tense		1st Conj.	2nd Conj.	3rd Conj.	3rd **io** Conj.	4th Conj.	Sum
Present	sing.	amo amas amat	móneo mones monet	rego regis regit	cápio capis capit	áudio audis audit	sum es est
	pl.	amamus amatis amant	monemus monetis monent	régimus régitis regunt	cápimus cápitis cápiunt	audimus auditis áudiunt	sumus estis sunt
Imperfect	sing.	amabam amabas amabat	monebam monebas monebat	regebam regebas regebat	capiebam capiebas capiebat	audiebam audiebas audiebat	eram eras erat
	pl.	amabamus amabatis amabant	monebamus monebatis monebant	regebamus regebatis regebant	capiebamus capiebatis capiebant	audiebamus audiebatis audiebant	eramus eratis erant
Future	sing.	amabo amabis amabit	monebo monebis monebit	regam reges reget	cápiam cápies cápiet	áudiam áudies áudiet	ero eris erit
	pl.	amábimus amábitis amabunt	monébimus monébitis monebunt	regemus regetis regent	capiemus capietis cápient	audiemus audietis áudient	érimus éritis erunt
Perfect	sing.	amavi amavisti amavit	mónui monuisti mónuit	rexi rexisti rexit	cepi cepisti cepit	audivi audivisti audivit	fui fuisti fuit
	pl.	amávimus amavistis amaverunt	monúimus monuistis monuerunt	réximus rexistis rexerunt	cépimus cepistis ceperunt	audívimus audivistis audiverunt	fúimus fuistis fuerunt
Pluperfect	sing.	amáveram amáveras amáverat	monúeram monúeras monúerat	réxeram réxeras réxerat	céperam céperas céperat	audíveram audíveras audíverat	fúeram fúeras fúerat
	pl.	amaveramus amaveratis amáverant	monueramus monueratis monúerant	rexeramus rexeratis réxerant	ceperamus ceperatis céperant	audiveramus audiveratis audíverant	fueramus fueratis fúerant
Future Perfect	sing.	amávero amáveris amáverit	monúero monúeris monúerit	réxero réxeris réxerit	cépero céperis céperit	audívero audíveris audíverit	fúero fúeris fúerit
	pl.	amavérimus amavéritis amáverint	monuérimus monuéritis monúerint	rexérimus rexéritis réxerint	cepérimus cepéritis céperint	audivérimus audivéritis audíverint	fúerimus fuéritis fúerint

Active Indicative Meanings

Tense	Number	1st Conj.	Sum
Present	sing.	I love, do love, am loving you love, do love, are loving he, she, it loves, does love, is loving	I am you are he, she, it is
	pl.	we love, do love, are loving you all love do love, are loving they love, do love, are loving	we are you all are they are
Imperfect	sing.	I was loving you were loving he, she, it was loving	I was you were he, she, it was
	pl.	we were loving you all were loving they were loving	we were you all were they were
Future	sing.	I will love you will love he, she, it will love	I will be you will be he, she, it will be
	pl.	we will love you all will love they will love	we will be you all will be they will be
Perfect	sing.	I loved, have loved, did love you loved, have loved, did love he, she, it loved, has loved, did love	I have been you have been he, she, it has been
	pl.	we loved, have loved, did love you all loved, have loved, did love they loved, have loved, did love	we have been you all have been they have been
Pluperfect	sing.	I had loved you had loved he, she, it had loved	I had been you had been he, she, it had been
	pl.	we had loved you all had loved they had loved	we had been you all had been they a had been re
Future Perfect	sing.	I will have loved you will have loved he, she, it will have loved	I will have been you will have been he, she, it will have been
	pl.	we will have loved you all will have loved they will have loved	we will have been you all will have been they will have been

Present System Passive Indicative of the Four Conjugations

Tense		1st Conj.	2nd Conj.	3rd Conj.	3rd **io** Conj.	4th Conj.
Present	sing.	amor amaris amatur	móneor moneris monetur	regor régeris régitur	cápior cáperis cápitur	áudior audiris auditur
	pl.	amamur amámini amantur	monemur monémini monentur	régimur regímini reguntur	cápimur capímini capiuntur	audimur audímini audiuntur
Imperfect	sing.	amabar amabaris amabatur	monebar monebaris monebatur	regebar regebaris regebatur	capiebar capiebaris capiebatur	audiebar audiebaris audiebatur
	pl.	amabamur amabámini amabantur	monebamur monebámini monebantur	regebamur regebámini regebantur	capiebamur capiebámini capiebantur	audiebamur audiebámini audiebantur
Future	sing.	amabor amáberis amábitur	monebor monéberis monébitur	regar regeris regetur	cápiar capieris capietur	áudiar audieris audietur
	pl.	amábimur amabímini amabuntur	monébimur monebímini monebuntur	regemur regémini regentur	capiemur capiémini capientur	audiemur audiémini audientur

Present System Passive Indicative Meanings

Tense	S.	Pl.
Present	I am loved, am being loved you are loved, are being loved he, she, it is loved, is being loved	we are loved, are being loved you all are loved, are being loved they are loved, are being loved
Imperfect	I was being loved you were being loved he, she, it was being loved	we were being loved you all were being loved they were being loved
Future	I will be loved you will be loved he, she, it will be loved	we will be loved you all will be loved they will be loved

103

Oral Form Drills

FOR LESSONS

II, III, V, IX, X
XI, XIII, XXII, XXVI

Lesson II

1.	cultrorum	1.	the boys (d.o.)
2.	púero	2.	to/for the men
3.	líberos	3.	the teacher's (f.)
4.	agrum	4.	of a knife
5.	parvo libro	5.	children
6.	multi viri	6.	third evening
7.	liberis	7.	to/for a good boy
8.	quinque púeri	8.	many knives (d.o.)
9.	decem magistros	9.	big fields
10.	quattuor libri	10.	of new books

Lesson III

1.	viros pigros	1.	sick horse (d.o.)
2.	púero mísero	2.	of a lazy dog
3.	virum dextrum	3.	to/for the free men
4.	librum pulchrum	4.	wretched days
5.	mílites íntegri	5.	left hand
6.	pede dextro	6.	beautiful houses
7.	cor ásperum	7.	harsh hearts
8.	viro líbero	8.	uninjured leader
9.	liber sacer	9.	to the lazy boys
10.	canem aegrum	10.	of harsh words

Lesson V

1.	navibus	1.	the sea (sub)
2.	montium	2.	of the hills
3.	partem	3.	to/for the seas
4.	maria	4.	ibwf the bridge
5.	montes	5.	citizens (d.o.)
6.	civibus	6.	citizens (sub.)
7.	urbium	7.	to/for the part
8.	mari	8.	of the navies
9.	colli	9.	of the tribe
10.	gentis	10.	to/for the enemies

Lesson IX

1.	pater noster	1.	my book
2.	nomen tuum	2.	my books
3.	regnum tuum	3.	our field
4.	panem nostrum	4.	our fields
5.	tua dona	5.	your window
6.	Dominun nostrum	6.	your windows
7.	mater mea	7.	your all's ship
8.	mater vestra	8.	your all's ships
9.	matres vestrae	9.	my head
10.	tui fratres	10.	our heads

Lesson X

1.	sub portā	1.	without anger
2.	in ínsulā	2.	out of the shadow
3.	pro provinciā	3.	for (the) good
4.	sine viis	4.	with us
5.	cum Lúciā	5.	from the city
6.	de Gálliā	6.	in the kitchen
7.	prae exercitu	7.	at the head of the harbor
8.	e stellis	8.	about the women
9.	coram Deo	9.	with you
10.	a mari	10.	with me

Lesson XI

1.	ob epístulas	1.	among the cows
2.	inter ursas	2.	against the fatherland
3.	per portam	3.	through the doors
4.	circum lunam	4.	onto the road
5.	in turbam	5.	between the farmhouses
6.	post cenam	6.	around the island
7.	sub aras	7.	before dawn
8.	contra jánuam	8.	near the window
9.	propter victóriam	9.	toward the gate
10.	trans provínciam	10.	after the story

Lesson XIII

1.	vivis	1.	they will join
2.	jungunt	2.	we will drag
3.	dicetis	3.	we build
4.	trahebamus	4.	you all will live
5.	struam	5.	she was leading
6.	véhitis	6.	you convey
7.	ducebat	7.	they were ruling
8.	regent	8.	I will say
9.	júngimus	9.	it leads
10.	strues	10.	they were building

Lesson XXII

1.	portatur	1.	we are greeted
2.	oppugnamur	2.	he is wounded
3.	culparis	3.	they are expected
4.	demonstrantur	4.	it is washed
5.	perturbatur	5.	they are given
6.	vulnerámini	6.	you all are loved
7.	mutatur	7.	we are blamed
8.	accusor	8.	they are helped
9.	creantur	9.	you are disturbed
10.	exploratur	10.	it is doubted

Lesson XXVI

11.	finitur	1.	I will be discovered
12.	impediebar	2.	she was being hindered
13.	sentientur	3.	they will be fortified
14.	scietur	4.	you all were being heard
15.	inveniuntur	5.	it is felt
16.	audímini	6.	it was being limited
17.	muniebatur	7.	it is known
18.	inveniemur	8.	you are being discovered
19.	audiar	9.	they were being hindered
20.	audiebaris	10.	it is not known

VOCABULARY
INDEX

a, ab	from, by	**caelum -i** *n.*	sky, heaven
accuso (1)	to accuse	**campus -i** *m.*	field, plain
ad	to, toward, at	**canis canis** *m. or f.*	dog
adoro (1)	to adore	**cápio -ere cepi captus**	to take, capture
adventus -ûs *m.*	arrival	**caput cápitis** *n.*	head
aeger aegra aegrum	sick, ill	**cáveo -ēre cavi cautus**	to be aware of,
aeternus, a, um	eternal, everlasting		guard against
ager agri *m.*	field, ground	**celo (1)**	to hide
agnus -i *m.*	lamb	**cena -ae** *f.*	dinner
agrícola -ae *m.*	farmer	**certē**	certainly
altē	highly, deeply	**certus, a, um**	certain
altus, a, um	high, deep	**Christianus -i** *m.*	a Christian
ámbulo (1)	to walk	**Christus -i** *m.*	Christ
amicus -i *m.*	friend	**cibus -i** *m.*	food
amo (1)	to love, like	**circum**	around
amor amoris *m.*	love, passion	**cívis civis** *m. or f.*	citizen
ánimus -i *m.*	mind, spirit	**clamo (1)**	to shout
annus -i *m.*	year	**clamor -oris** *m.*	shout, cry
ante	before (in time and place)	**collis collis** *m.*	hill
appáreo (2)	to appear	**collum -i** *n.*	neck
appello (1)	to address	**contra**	against
apud	among	**cor cordis** *n.*	heart
aqua -ae *f.*	water	**coram**	in the presence of
áquila -ae *f.*	eagle	**corona -ae** *f.*	crown
ara -ae *f.*	altar	**cras**	tomorrow
arbor árboris *f.*	tree	**creo (1)**	to create
árdeo -ēre arsi arsus	to burn, be on fire	**crux crucis** *f.*	cross
argentum -i *n.*	silver	**culina -ae** *f.*	kitchen
aro (1)	to plow	**culpa -ae** *f.*	fault, blame
asper áspera ásperum	sharp, harsh	**culpo (1)**	to blame
asperē	roughly	**culter cultri** *m.*	knife
áudio (4)	to hear	**cum**	with
aurora -ae *f.*	dawn	**cúpio -ere -ivi -itus**	to desire, wish for
aurum -i *n.*	gold	**cur?**	why?
bárbarus -i *m.*	barbarian, foreigner	**de**	about, down from
bellum -i *n.*	war	**débeo (2)**	to owe, ought
bonus, a, um	good	**débitum -i** *n.*	debt, sin
brácchium -i *n.*	arm (forearm)	**decem**	ten
brevis, e	short, brief	**décimus, a, um**	tenth
bréviter	shortly, briefly	**delecto (1)**	to delight, please

demonstro (1)	to show, point out
deus -i *m.*	god
dexter dextra dextrum	right, right-hand
dico -ere dixi dictus	to say, tell
dies -ei *m.*	day
difficíliter	with difficulty
diffícilis, e	difficult
discípulus -i *m.*	student
do dare dedi datus	to give
dóceo -ēre dócui doctus	to teach
dolor -oris *m.*	grief, pain
dóminus -i *m.*	lord, master
domus -ūs *f.*	house, home
donum -i *n.*	gift
dórmio -ire -ivi -itus	to sleep
dúbito (1)	to doubt
duco -ere duxi ductus	to lead
dulcis, e	sweet, pleasant
duo -ae -o	two
dux ducis *m.*	leader
e, ex	out of, out from
ego mei	I, me
epístula -ae *f.*	letter
equus -i *m.*	horse
erro (1)	to err, wander
exércitus -ūs *m.*	army
exploro (1)	to explore
exspecto (1)	to wait for, expect
fábula -ae *f.*	story, tale
fácies -ei *f.*	face
fácile	easily
fácilis, e	easy
fácio -ere feci factus	to make, do
fémina -ae *f.*	woman
fenestra -ae *f.*	window
ferrum -i *n.*	iron, iron tool
fidéliter	faithfully
fidelis, e	faithful
fides fídei *f.*	faith, trust
figo -ere fixi fictus	to fix, fasten
fília -ae *f.*	daughter
fílius -i *m.*	son
fínio (4)	to finish, limit
flumen flúminis *n.*	river
fólium -i *n.*	leaf
fórtiter	bravely
fortis, e	strong, brave
fortuna -ae *f.*	fortune
forum -i *n.*	forum, marketplace
frater fratris *m.*	brother
fructus -ūs *m.*	fruit
frumentum -i *n.*	grain, corn
fúgio -ere fugi fúgitus	to flee
Gállia -ae *f.*	Gaul
Gallus -i *m.*	a Gaul
gáudeo -ēre -- --	to rejoice
gáudium -i *n.*	joy
gens gentis *f.*	tribe
gládius -i *m.*	sword
grátia -ae *f.*	grace, favor, thanks (pl.)
gráviter	heavily
gravis, e	heavy, serious, severe
hábeo (2)	to have
hábito (1)	to live in, dwell
herba -ae *f.*	green plant, grass
heri	yesterday
Hispánia -ae *f.*	Spain
hódie	today
hortus -i *m.*	garden
hostis hostis *m. or f.*	enemy
impédio (4)	to hinder, obstruct
imperator -oris *m.*	general, commander
in (w/ abl.)	in, on
in (w/ acc.)	into, onto
ínsula -ae *f.*	island
ínteger -gra -grum	whole, uninjured
inter	between
invénio -ire -veni -ventus	to discover, find out
ira -ae *f.*	anger

Itália -ae *f.*	Italy	máneo -ēre mansi -sus	to remain, stay
jácio -ere jeci jactus	to throw, hurl	manus -ūs *f.*	hand
jánua -ae *f.*	door	Marcus -i *m.*	Mark
júbeo -ēre jussi jussus	to order	mare maris *n.*	sea
júdico (1)	to judge, consider	Maria -ae *f.*	Mary
jungo -ere junxi junctus	to join, connect	mater matris *f.*	mother
juvo -are juvi jutus	to help	mensa -ae *f.*	table
juxta	near	metus -ūs *m.*	fear
labor -oris *m.*	work, toil	meus -a -um	my
laboro (1)	to work	miles mílitis *m.*	soldier
lacus -ūs *m.*	lake	miser mísera míserum	wretched
laetē	happily	miserē	unhappily
laetus, a, um	happy	móneo (2)	to warn
latē	widely	mons montis *m.*	mountain
latus, a, um	wide, broad	mos moris *m.*	custom
laudo (1)	to praise	móveo -ēre movi motus	to move
lavo -are lavi lautus	to wash	multus, a, um	much, many
legatus -i *m.*	lieutenant	mundus -i *m.*	world, mankind
lentē	slowly	múnio (4)	to fortify, protect
lentus, a, um	slow	muto (1)	to change
lex legis *f.*	law	narro (1)	to tell
liber líbera líberum	free	nato (1)	to swim
liber libri *m.*	book	nauta -ae *m.*	sailor
liberē	freely	návigo (1)	to sail
líberi -orum *m.*	children	navis navis *f.*	ship
líbero (1)	free, to set free	nego (1)	to deny
lignum -i *n.*	wood	néscio (4)	to not know
locus -i *m.*	place	nimbus -i *m.*	cloud, storm cloud
longē	far, by far	nóbilis, e	noble
longus, a, um	long	nomen nóminis *n.*	name
Lúcia -ae *f.*	Lucy	non	not
ludus -i *m.*	game, school	nonus, a, um	ninth
lumen lúminis *n.*	lamp	nos nostri	we
luna -ae *f.*	moon	noster nostra nostrum	our
lupus -i *m.*	wolf	novem	nine
lux lucis *f.*	light	novus, a, um	new
magister magistri *m.*	teacher (male)	numquam	never
magistra -ae *f.*	teacher (female)	nunc	now
magnus, a, um	great, large	núntio (1)	to report
malus, a, um	bad	ob	because of

óccupo (1)	to seize	província -ae *f.*	province
octavus, a, um	eighth	puella -ae *f.*	girl
octo	eight	puer -i *m.*	boy, child
óculus -i *m.*	eye	pugno (1)	to fight
omnis, e	each, every (s.), all (pl.)	pulcher -chra -chrum	beautiful
óppidum -i *n.*	town	pulchrē	beautifully
oppugno (1)	to attack	puto (1)	to think
opto (1)	to desire, wish	quam diu?	how long?
orator -oris *m.*	speaker, orator	quando?	when?
oro (1)	to speak, pray	quartus, a, um	fourth
panis panis *m.*	bread	quattuor	four
paro (1)	to prepare	quid?	what?
pars partis *f.*	part, region	quinque	five
parvus, a, um	small	quintus, a, um	fifth
pastor -oris *m.*	shepherd, pastor	quis?	who?
pater patris *m.*	father	quomodo?	how?
pátria -ae *f.*	fatherland, country	quot?	how many?
pax pacis *f.*	peace	regina -ae *f.*	queen
peccatum -i *n.*	sin, mistake	regnum -i *n.*	kingdom
pecúnia -ae *f.*	money	rego -ere rexi rectus	to rule
per	through	res -ei *f.*	thing, matter, affair, business
perturbo (1)	to disturb		
pes pedis *m.*	foot	respóndeo -ēre -di -sus	to respond
piger pigra pigrum	lazy	rex regis *m.*	king
piscator -oris *m.*	fisherman	rogo (1)	to ask
poeta -ae *m.*	poet	Roma -ae *f.*	Rome
pons pontis *m.*	bridge	Romanus -i *m.*	a Roman
pópulus -i *m.*	people	sacer sacra sacrum	sacred
porta -ae *f.*	gate	sáeculum -i *n.*	age, time period
porto (1)	to carry	saepe	often
portus -ūs *m.*	harbor	saluto (1)	to greet
post	after, behind	sanctus, a, um	sacred, holy
prae	at the head of	saxum -i *n.*	rock
práemium -i *n.*	reward	scio (4)	to know
primus, a, um	first	scutum -i *n.*	shield
pro	for, on behalf of, in front of	secundus, a, um	second
		sédeo -ēre sedi sessus	to sit
próelium -i *n.*	battle	sella -ae *f.*	seat
prohíbeo (2)	to prevent	semper	always
propter	on account of	senator -oris *m.*	senator

senatus -ūs *m.*	senate	**trans**	across
séntio -ire sensi sensus	to feel, perceive	**tres**	three
septem	seven	**tu tui**	you
séptimus, a, um	seventh	**tum**	then, at that time
servo (1)	to guard, keep	**turba -ae** *f.*	crowd, turmoil
servus -i *m.*	slave, servant	**túrpiter**	shamefully
sex	six	**turpis, e**	shameful, disgraceful
sextus, a, um	sixth	**tuus -a -um**	your (s.)
signum -i *n.*	sign	**ubi?**	where, in what place?
silva -ae *f.*	forest	**umbra -ae** *f.*	shadow
sine	without	**umquam**	ever
sinister -tra -trum	left, left-hand	**unda -ae** *f.*	wave
sócius -i *m.*	ally	**unus, a, um**	one
sol solis *m.*	sun	**urbs urbis** *f.*	city
soror sororis *f.*	sister	**ursa -ae** *f.*	bear
specto (1)	to look at	**vacca -ae** *f.*	cow
spero (1)	to hope	**váleo -ēre válui --**	to be strong, be well
spes -ei *f.*	hope	**vallum -i** *n.*	wall, rampart
spíritus -ūs *m.*	spirit	**veho -ere vexi vectus**	to carry, convey,
stella -ae *f.*	star		transport
sto stare steti status	to stand	**vénio -ire veni ventus**	to come
struo -ere -uxi -uctus	to build, construct	**ventus -i** *m.*	wind
stúdium -i *n.*	zeal, enthusiasm, study	**verbum -i** *n.*	word
sub (with abl.)	under, at the foot of	**vesper vésperi** *m.*	evening
sub (with acc.)	to the foot of	**vester vestra vestrum**	your (pl.)
sum esse fui futurus	to be	**via -ae** *f.*	road, way
súpero (1)	to overcome	**victória -ae** *f.*	victory
tabella -ae *f.*	writing tablet	**vídeo -ēre vidi visus**	to see
táceo (2)	to be silent	**villa -ae** *f.*	farmhouse
telum -i *n.*	missile (javelin, spear)	**vinco -ere vici victus**	to conquer
templum -i *n.*	temple	**vinum -i** *n.*	wine
tempto (1)	to tempt	**vir viri** *m.*	man
téneo -ēre ténui tentus	to hold	**vita -ae** *f.*	life
tenus	as far as	**vivo -ere vixi victus**	to live, be alive
tergum -i *n.*	back, rear	**voco (1)**	to call
terra -ae *f.*	earth, land	**volo (1)**	to fly
térreo (2)	to frighten	**vos vestri**	you all
tértius, a, um	third	**vox vocis** *f.*	voice
tímeo -ēre tímui --	to fear, be afraid of	**vúlnero (1)**	to wound
traho -ere traxi tractus	to drag, haul		

about	**de**	beautifully	**pulchrē**
accuse	**accuso (1)**	because of	**ob**
across	**trans**	before (in time and place)	**ante**
address	**appello (1)**	behind	**post**
adore	**adoro (1)**	between	**inter**
affair	**res -ei** *f.*	blame (noun)	**culpa -ae** *f.*
after	**post**	blame (verb)	**culpo (1)**
against	**contra**	book	**liber libri** *m.*
age	**sáeculum -i** *n.*	boy	**puer -i** *m.*
all	**omnis, e**	brave	**fortis, e**
ally	**sócius -i** *m.*	bravely	**fórtiter**
altar	**ara -ae** *f.*	bread	**panis panis** *m.*
always	**semper**	bridge	**pons pontis** *m.*
among	**apud**	brief	**brevis, e**
anger	**ira -ae** *f.*	briefly	**bréviter**
appear	**appáreo (2)**	broad	**latus, a, um**
arm	**brácchium -i** *n.*	brother	**frater fratris** *m.*
army	**exércitus -ūs** *m.*	build	**struo -ere struxi structus**
around	**circum**	burn	**árdeo -ēre arsi arsus**
arrival	**adventus -ūs** *m.*	business	**res -ei** *f.*
as far as	**tenus**	by	**a, ab**
ask	**rogo (1)**	by far	**longē**
at	**ad**	call	**voco (1)**
at that time	**tum**	capture	**cápio capere cepi captus**
at the foot of	**sub (with abl.)**	carry	**porto (1); veho -ere**
at the head of	**prae**	certain	**certus, a, um**
attack	**oppugno (1)**	certainly	**certē**
back	**tergum -i** *n.*	change	**muto (1)**
bad	**malus, a, um**	child	**puer -i** *m.*
barbarian	**bárbarus -i** *m.*	children	**líberi -orum** *m.*
battle	**próelium -i** *n.*	Christ	**Christus -i** *m.*
be	**sum esse fui futurus**	Christian (adj.)	**Christianus, a, um**
be afraid of	**tímeo -ēre tímui**	Christian (noun)	**Christianus -i** *m.*
be alive	**vivo -ere vixi victus**	citizen	**civis -is** *m. or f.*
be aware of	**cáveo -ēre cavi cautus**	city	**urbs urbis** *f.*
be on fire	**árdeo -ēre arsi arsus**	cloud	**nimbus -i** *m.*
be silent	**táceo (2)**	come	**vénio -ire veni ventus**
be strong	**váleo -ēre válui --**	commander	**imperator -oris** *m.*
be well	**váleo -ēre válui --**	connect	**jungo -ere junxi junctus**
bear	**ursa -ae** *f.*	conquer	**vinco -ere vici victus**
beautiful	**pulcher -chra -chrum**	construct	**struo -ere struxi structus**

convey	**veho -ere**	err	**erro (1)**
corn	**frumentum -i** *n.*	eternal	**aeternus, a, um**
country	**pátria -ae** *f.*	evening	**vesper vesperi** *m.*
cow	**vacca -ae** *f.*	ever	**umquam**
create	**creo (1)**	everlasting	**aeternus, a, um**
cross	**crux crucis** *f.*	every	**omnis, e**
crowd	**turba -ae** *f.*	expect	**exspecto (1)**
crown	**corona -ae** *f.*	explore	**exploro (1)**
cry	**clamor -oris** *m.*	eye	**óculus -i** *m.*
custom	**mos moris** *m.*	face	**fácies -ei** *f.*
dart	**telum -i** *n.*	faith	**fides fídei** *f.*
daughter	**fília -ae** *f.*	faithful	**fidelis, e**
dawn	**aurora -ae** *f.*	faithfully	**fidéliter**
day	**dies -ei** *m.*	far	**longē**
debt	**débitum -i** *n.*	farmer	**agrícola -ae** *m.*
deep	**altus, a, um**	farmhouse	**villa -ae** *f.*
deeply	**altē**	fasten	**figo -ere**
delight	**delecto (1)**	father	**pater patris** *m.*
deny	**nego (1)**	fatherland	**pátria -ae** *f.*
desire	**cúpio -ere -ivi –itus; opto (1)**	fault	**culpa -ae** *f.*
difficult	**diffícilis, e**	favor	**grátia -ae** *f.*
dinner	**cena -ae** *f.*	fear (noun)	**metus -ūs** *m.*
discover	**invénio -ire -veni -ventus**	fear (verb)	**tímeo -ēre tímui --**
disgraceful	**turpis, e**	feel	**séntio -ire sensi sensus**
disturb	**perturbo (1)**	field	**ager agri** *m.*; **campus -i** *m.*
do	**fácio -ere feci factus**	fifth	**quintus, a, um**
dog	**canis canis** *m. or f.*	fight	**pugno (1)**
door	**jánua -ae** *f.*	find out	**invénio -ire -veni -ventus**
doubt	**dúbito (1)**	finish	**fínio -ire -ivi -itus**
down from	**de**	first	**primus, a, um**
drag	**traho -ere traxi tractus**	fisherman	**piscator -oris** *m.*
dwell	**hábito (1)**	five	**quinque**
each	**omnis, e**	fix	**figo -ere fixi fictus**
eagle	**áquila -ae** *f.*	flee	**fúgio -ere fugi fúgitus**
earth	**terra -ae** *f.*	fly	**volo (1)**
easy	**fácilis, e**	food	**cibus -i** *m.*
easily	**fácile**	foot	**pes pedis** *m.*
eight	**octo**	for	**pro**
eighth	**octavus, a, um**	foreigner	**bárbarus -i** *m.*
enemy	**hostis hostis** *m. or f.*	forest	**silva -ae** *f.*
enthusiasm	**stúdium -i** *n.*	fortify	**múnio -ire -ivi -itus**

fortune	**fortuna -ae** *f.*	hear	**áudio (4)**
forum	**forum -i** *n.*	heart	**cor cordis** *n.*
four	**quattuor**	heaven	**caelum -i** *n.*
fourth	**quartus, a, um**	heavy	**gravis, e**
free (adj.)	**liber líbera líberum**	heavily	**gráviter**
free (verb)	**líbero (1)**	help	**juvo -are juvi jutus**
freely	**liberē**	hide	**celo (1)**
friend	**amicus -i** *m.*	high	**altus, a, um**
frighten	**térreo (2)**	highly	**altē**
from	**a, ab**	hill	**collis collis** *m.*
fruit	**fructus -ūs** *m.*	hinder	**impédio (4)**
game	**ludus -i** *m.*	hold	**téneo -ēre ténui tentus**
garden	**hortus -i** *m.*	holy	**sanctus, a, um**
gate	**porta -ae** *f.*	home	**domus -ūs** *f.*
a Gaul	**Gallus -i** *m.*	hope (noun)	**spes -ei** *f.*
Gaul	**Gállia -ae** *f.*	hope (verb)	**spero (1)**
general	**imperator -oris** *m.*	horse	**equus -i** *m.*
gift	**donum -i** *n.*	house	**domus -ūs** *f.*
girl	**puella -ae** *f.*	how?	**quomodo?**
give	**do dare dedi datus**	how long?	**quam diu?**
god	**deus -i** *m.*	how many?	**quot?**
gold	**aurum -i** *n.*	hurl	**jácio -ere jeci jactus**
good	**bonus, a, um**	I	**ego**
grace	**grátia -ae** *f.*	ill	**aeger aegra aegrum**
grain	**frumentum -i** *n.*	in	**in (w/ abl.)**
grass	**herba -ae** *f.*	in front of	**pro**
great	**magnus, a, um**	in the presence of	**coram**
green plant	**herba -ae** *f.*	into	**in (w/ acc.)**
greet	**saluto (1)**	iron, iron tool	**ferrum -i** *n.*
grief	**dolor -oris** *m.*	island	**ínsula -ae** *f.*
ground	**ager agri** *m.*	Italy	**Itália -ae** *f.*
guard	**servo (1)**	javelin	**telum -i** *n.*
guard against	**cáveo -ēre cavi cautus**	join	**jungo -ere junxi junctus**
hand	**manus -ūs** *f.*	joy	**gáudium -i** *n.*
happy	**laetus, a, um**	judge	**júdico (1)**
happily	**laetē**	keep	**servo (1)**
harbor	**portus -ūs** *m.*	king	**rex regis** *m.*
harsh	**asper áspera ásperum**	kingdom	**regnum -i** *n.*
haul	**traho -ere traxi tractus**	kitchen	**culina -ae** *f.*
have	**hábeo (2)**	knife	**culter cultri** *m.*
head	**caput cápitis** *n.*	know	**scio (4)**

lake	**lacus -ūs** *m.*	mother	**mater matris** *f.*
lamb	**agnus -i** *m.*	mountain	**mons montis** *m.*
lamp	**lumen lúminis** *n.*	move	**móveo -ēre movi motus**
land	**terra -ae** *f.*	much	**multus, a, um**
large	**magnus, a, um**	my	**meus, a, um**
law	**lex legis** *f.*	name	**nomen nóminis** *n.*
lazy	**piger pigra pigrum**	near	**juxta**
lead	**duco -ere duxi ductus**	neck	**collum -i** *n.*
leader	**dux ducis** *m.*	never	**numquam**
leaf	**fólium -i** *m.*	new	**novus, a, um**
learning	**stúdium -i** *n.*	nine	**novem**
left, left-hand	**sinister sinistra sinistrum**	ninth	**nonus, a, um**
letter	**epístula -ae** *f.*	noble	**nóbilis, e**
lieutenant	**legatus -i** *m.*	not	**non**
life	**vita -ae** *f.*	not know	**néscio (4)**
light	**lux lucis** *f.*	now	**nunc**
like	**amo (1)**	obstruct	**impédio (4)**
limit	**fínio (4)**	often	**saepe**
live	**vivo -ere vixi victus**	on	**in (w/ abl.)**
live in	**hábito (1)**	on account of	**propter**
long	**longus, a, um**	on behalf of	**pro**
look at	**specto (1)**	one	**unus, a, um**
lord	**dóminus -i** *m.*	onto	**in (w/ acc.)**
love (noun)	**amor amoris** *m.*	orator	**orator -oris** *m.*
love (verb)	**amo (1)**	order	**júbeo -ēre jussi jussus**
Lucy	**Lúcia -ae** *f.*	ought	**débeo (2)**
make	**fácio -ere feci factus**	out from, out of	**e, ex**
man	**vir viri** *m.*	overcome	**súpero (1)**
mankind	**mundus -i** *m.*	owe	**débeo (2)**
many	**multus, a, um**	pain	**dolor -oris** *m.*
Mark	**Marcus -i** *m.*	part	**pars partis** *f.*
marketplace	**forum -i** *n.*	passion	**amor amoris** *m.*
Mary	**Maria -ae** *f.*	pastor	**pastor -oris** *m.*
master	**dóminus -i** *m.*	peace	**pax pacis** *f.*
matter	**res -ei** *f.*	people	**pópulus -i** *m.*
me	**mei mihi me**	perceive	**séntio -ire sensi sensus**
mind	**ánimus -i** *m.*	place (noun)	**locus -i** *m.*
missile	**telum -i** *n.*	plain	**campus -i** *m.*
mistake	**peccatum -i** *n.*	pleasant	**dulcis, e**
money	**pecúnia -ae** *f.*	please	**delecto (1)**
moon	**luna -ae** *f.*	plow	**aro (1)**

poet	poeta -ae *m.*	seriously	graviter
point out	demonstro (1)	servant	servus -i *m.*
praise	laudo (1)	set free	líbero (1)
pray	oro (1)	seven	septem
prepare	paro (1)	severe	gravis, e
prevent	prohíbeo (2)	seventh	séptimus, a, um
protect	múnio (4)	shadow	umbra -ae *f.*
province	província -ae *f.*	shameful	turpis, e
queen	regina -ae *f.*	shamefully	túrpiter
rampart	vallum -i *n.*	sharp	asper áspera ásperum
rear	tergum -i *n.*	shepherd	pastor -oris *m.*
region	pars partis *f.*	shield	scutum -i *n.*
rejoice	gáudeo -ēre -- --	ship	navis navis *f.*
remain	máneo -ēre mansi -sus	short	brevis, e
report	núntio (1)	shortly	bréviter
respond	respondeo -ēre respondi	shout	clamo (1)
	responsus	shout	clamor -oris *m.*
reward	práemium -i *n.*	show	demonstro (1)
right, right-hand	dexter dextra dextrum	sick	aeger aegra aegrum
river	flumen flúminis *n.*	sign	signum -i *n.*
road	via -ae *f.*	silver	argentum -i *n.*
rock	saxum -i *n.*	sin	débitum -i *n.*; peccatum -i *n.*
Roman (adj.)	Romanus, a, um	sister	soror sororis *f.*
Roman (noun)	Romanus -i *m.*	sit	sédeo -ēre sedi sessus
Rome	Roma -ae *f.*	six	sex
roughly	asperē	sixth	sextus, a, um
rule	rego -ere rexi rectus	sky	caelum -i *n.*
sacred	sanctus, a, um;	slave	servus -i *m.*
	sacer sacra sacrum	sleep	dórmio -ire -ivi -itus
sail	návigo (1)	slow	lentus, a, um
sailor	nauta -ae *m.*	slowly	lentē
say	dico -ere dixi dictus	small	parvus, a, um
school	ludus -i *m.*	soldier	miles mílitis *m.*
sea	mare maris *n.*	son	fílius -i *m.*
seat	sella -ae *f.*	Spain	Hispánia -ae *f.*
second	secundus, a, um	speak	oro (1)
see	vídeo -ēre vidi visus	speaker	orator -oris *m.*
seize	óccupo (1)	spear	telum -i *n.*
senate	senatus -ūs *m.*	spirit	ánimus -i *m.*; spíritus -ūs *m.*
senator	senator -oris *m.*	stand	sto stare steti status
serious	gravis, e	star	stella -ae *f.*

stay	**máneo -ēre mansi -sus**	trust	**fides -ei** *f.*
storm cloud	**nimbus -i** *m.*	turmoil	**turba -ae** *f.*
story	**fábula -ae** *f.*	two	**duo -ae -o**
strong	**fortis, e**	unhappily	**miserē**
student	**discípulus -i** *m.*	uninjured	**ínteger íntegra íntegrum**
study	**stúdium -i** *n.*	under	**sub (with abl. or acc.)**
sun	**sol solis** *m.*	victory	**victória -ae** *f.*
sweet	**dulcis, e**	voice	**vox vocis** *f.*
swim	**nato (1)**	wait for	**exspecto (1)**
sword	**gládius -i** *m.*	walk	**ámbulo (1)**
table	**mensa -ae** *f.*	wall	**vallum -i** *n.*
take	**cápio -ere cepi captus**	wander	**erro (1)**
tale	**fábula -ae** *f.*	war	**bellum -i** *n.*
teach	**dóceo -ēre dócui doctus**	warn	**móneo (2)**
teacher (male)	**magister magistri** *m.*	wash	**lavo -are lavi lautus**
teacher (female)	**magistra -ae** *f.*	water	**aqua -ae** *f.*
tell	**dico -ere dixi dictus;**	wave	**unda -ae** *f.*
	narro (1)	way	**via -ae** *f.*
temple	**templum -i** *n.*	we	**nos nostri**
tempt	**tempto (1)**	what?	**quid?**
ten	**decem**	when?	**quando?**
tenth	**décimus, a, um**	where?	**ubi?**
thanks	**grátiae -arum** *f.*	who?	**quis?**
then	**tum**	whole	**ínteger íntegra íntegrum**
thing	**res -ei** *f.*	why?	**cur?**
think	**puto (1)**	wide	**latus, a, um**
third	**tértius, a, um**	widely	**latē**
three	**tres**	will	**voluntas -tatis** *f.*
through	**per**	wind	**ventus -i** *m.*
throw	**jácio -ere jeci jactus**	window	**fenestra -ae** *f.*
time period	**sáeculum -i** *n.*	wine	**vinum -i** *n.*
to	**ad**	wish	**opto (1)**
to the foot of	**sub (with acc.)**	wish for	**cupio -ere -ivi -itus**
today	**hódie**	with	**cum**
toil	**labor laboris** *m.*	with difficulty	**difficíliter**
tomorrow	**cras**	without	**sine**
toward	**ad**	wolf	**lupus -i** *m.*
town	**óppidum -i** *n.*	woman	**fémina -ae** *f.*
transport	**veho -ere**	wood	**lignum -i** *n.*
tree	**arbor árboris** *f.*	word	**verbum -i** *n.*
tribe	**gens gentis** *f.*	work (noun)	**labor laboris** *m.*

VOCABULARY: ENGLISH-LATIN

work (verb)	**laboro (1)**
world	**mundus -i** *m.*
wound	**vúlnero (1)**
wretched	**miser mísera míserum**
writing tablet	**tabella -ae** *f.*
year	**annus -i** *m.*
yesterday	**heri**
you	**tu tui**
you all	**vos vestri**
your	**tuus -a -um**
zeal	**stúdium -i** *n.*